DELICIOUS MIGRATION

STREET FOOD IN A GLOBALIZED WORLD

EDITORS

MARTINA KALLER, JOHN KEAR, AND MARKUS MAYER

1st Edition

2017

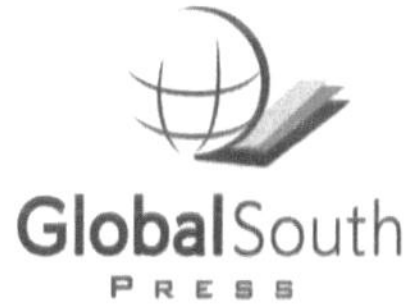

Global South
PRESS

DELICIOUS MIGRATION

By KALLER, Martina KEAR, John and MAYER, Markus

—1ˢᵗ ed. — 2017

Includes bibliographical references and index.

ISBN: 978-1-943350-43-8

1. International Studies — Globalization

2. Social Sciences — Emigration & Immigration

3. Cooking — Regional & Ethnic

Table of Contents

1. Acknowledgement vii

2. Contributors ix

3. Tasteful Contributions
John Kear, and Markus Mayer 13

4. Street Food: A Mobile Concept
Martina Kaller, John Kear, and Markus Mayer 17

5. Stirring the Melting Pot: Ethno-narcissistic
Cuisine and Surging Immigration in
Contemporary Spain
Iván Ovejero 47

6. Fetish, Nation-building and Hummus:
The Fetishization of Street Food throughout
Israel's Nation-building Process
Martina Salakova 61

7. Americanized Taco: A Mere Adjustment
of the Mexican Cuisine in Los Angeles's Palate?
Julia Rott 73

8. The Death of the Würstelstand:
Turkish Migration and Austrian Resistance as
Seen through the Microcosm of Street Food
in Vienna's Twentieth District
Rachel Kaye 91

9. Hidden Comeback: The Impact of the
Yugoslavian Guestworkers on Street
Food Habits in Vienna
Heinz Kriz 107

10. Kurdish Mussels on the Bosporus:
How Immigration, Street Food, and
Urban Planning Meet in Istanbul
Nicolas Horky 125

11. Norway's Street Food on Wheels: Gourmet
Food Trucks and Swedish Influence in Oslo
Kine Ariela Hemli 145

12. Sichuan-flavored Beef Noodle Soup
in Taipei: Its Origin and Process of
Becoming Popular in Taiwan
Wang Jin 163

13. Eating London's Street Food, 1603-1714:
Eel Pie, Pease Pottage and the Restoration
Emily Arthy 177

14. Index 192

Acknowledgement

The contributors to this volume include young scholars of global studies and global history who have pursued master's studies at the University of Vienna. Though their research was conducted under my supervision, the writing and editing processes were coordinated and guided by their colleagues: John Kear and Markus Mayer. They additionally took over the editing of the articles and wrote the introduction together with me. I give my respectful thanks to them and very much appreciate their dedication to the project as well as their endurance in finishing it.

Jaslyn Dugmore and Jake Friedly helped turn our global mumbo-jumbo into proper English by respecting the individual choice of each author to opt for British or American English.

We would like to thank Christian Navas, our publisher at GlobalSouth Press, for the opportunity to present our manuscript to the board in addition to his friendly and professional support.

The Erasmus Mundus European Master's in Global Studies at University of Vienna sponsored the printing costs of this volume. Our sincere thanks go to Meggi Grandner and Poldi Kögler, who encouraged us in our determination to publish this book.

Martina Kaller
Stanford, October 2016

Contributors

Emily ARTHY is currently in her final semester of studies in the M.A. Global History und Global Studies program at the University of Vienna.

Jaslyn DUGMORE is a Master of Dietetics Student at the University of Queensland, Brisbane expecting to graduate mid-2017. She was a student at the University of Vienna during an exchange semester as part of her Bachelor of Nutrition over the winter of 2014/2015.

Jake FRIEDLY is an American student who has been awarded a dual Master's degree from the University of Vienna and Leipzig University in March 2016 after participating in the Erasmus Mundus Global Studies program. A student of history. His thesis, "A Serious Failure: News, Satire, and the 2003 Invasion of Iraq," blends contemporary history with media theory.

Kine Ariela HEMLI is an Archaeology and Science and Technology Studies student at the Norwegian University for Science and Technology. Her work on Food History and Global History took place during an Erasmus stay in Vienna, Austria in the fall of 2014.

Nicolas HORKY is pursuing a M.A. in Global History & Global Studies at the University of Vienna where he also completed his bachelor degree at the department of Development Studies.

Martina KALLER is a professor of global history with a focus on global food history at the University of Vienna where she belongs to the core faculty of Global Studies—A European Perspective (Erasmus Mundus 2005–15).

Rachel KAYE graduated from the University of Vienna in 2015. Her Master's thesis, titled, "External Pressure or a Process from

Within: Austrian Restitution Policies in a Global Context 1994–2001," which explores Austrian politics, identity, and restitution.

John KEAR graduated with highest distinction from Duke University in 2013. His participation in the project coincided with the completion of his M.A. degree as a part of the Erasmus Mundus Global Studies program at the University of Vienna.

Heinz KRIZ is a History student at the University of Vienna and graduate agent of tourism and hospitality. His work on food history and global history took place in an issue-specific project course in Vienna, Austria in the fall of 2014.

Markus MAYER is currently in the final semester of his M.A. in History at the University of Vienna. His studies focus on late medieval and early modern history and included two years abroad in Cork (Ireland) and Paris.

Ivan OVEJERO is a second-year student in the European Master in Global Studies at the University of Vienna.

Martina SALAKOVA has studied in Linz, Zagreb, and Vienna and is currently pursuing her master's degree of Global History at the University of Vienna.

Julia ROTT is a Global History and Global Studies M.A. student at the University of Vienna.

WANG Jin was conferred a B.A. of English by Sichuan International Studies University in 2009. He participated in the making of the multi-award winning documentaries during his undergraduate. Jin finished the Erasmus Mundus Global Studies M.A. program at the University of Leipzig and the University of Vienna. His master's thesis is titled "Global Citizenship in Baha'i Faith: A Case Study of Baha'is in Vienna."

Tasteful Contributions

John Kear and Markus Mayer

We begin this book by first delving into the theories and concepts related to the phenomenon of street food by way of our introduction: "Street Food: a Mobile concept." By surveying the current field of research, we establish the place and role of this volume in food studies and migration studies. We also introduce additional examples and questions with the invitation of further reflection and research on the oft-neglected topic of street food.

Iván Ovejero provides the opening contribution to this volume with his article "Stirring the Melting Pot" in which he provides a theoretical framework on the influences and the consequences of migration on street food and national cuisine in general. To explain his concept of an ethno-narcissistic cuisine he uses the example of Spain, a country, which has dealt with large amounts of immigration from the year 2000 onwards. Therefore, Spain presents a tremendous example of how different ethnic groups use food as an ethnic marker and how we can find a hybridization and so adaption of a former "national" cuisine.

In her article, "Fetish, Nation-Building, and Hummus," Martina Salakova introduces the case of Israel, a country seeking to establish its national identity amidst the voices of multiple, oft competing, constituent characters. In this process, food plays a major role as the subject of constant fetishization. Salakova explains this process and provides an example of how important food in general, and street food specifically, is as an expression of cultural identity.—He highlights that cultural identity as a marker reflects common sense and cannot be comprehensively explained in an academic setting.

The theoretical framework Ovejero and Salakova present builds the foundation for approaching the next article, "Americanized

Taco," by Julia Rott. Los Angeles is a hotspot of Hispanic immigration in the United States, and it is no surprise that the city presents an enormous biotope for hybridization and the adaption of various cuisines. To deal with the huge amount of different dishes found in this melting pot, Julia Rott decides to focus on a specific and well-known product—the taco. She shows how this dish mirrors the shaping of an urban society by its ethnic groups and how the processes of integration and adaption to a new society work.

An ocean away from Los Angeles, Rachel Kaye leads us to the Austrian capital of Vienna and uses a polemic newspaper headline to examine how people from this city react to the rise of Turkish Kebab grills all over the city in her article "Death of the Würstelstand." She focuses on the Twentieth District of Vienna, one of the main hotspots of Turkish migration in the city. Through various methods, including a small survey, she tries to unveil, why the Kebab is seen as such a threat towards what are considered traditional forms of Viennese street food. In addition, she analyzes official statistics to question if Vienna really is facing the death of the Würstelstand.

A rather different situation can be found in the case of the impact of the Gastarbeiter migration to Austria. In his article "Hidden Comeback," Heinz Kriz examines the effect of the Balkan cuisine in Vienna in the 1970s and 1980s, highlighting the fact that many of the perceived new dishes are a well know part of the Viennese cuisine. Kriz asks why the guest workers had, compared to their large number, a relatively modest impact on street food in the city. Quickly we discover that many of the dishes the migrants brought with them fit well into the established milieu of the Viennese sausage stands.

A rather classical example for a city where street food has an evident importance is presented by Nicolas Horky in his article "Kurdish Mussels at the Bosporus." Istanbul has faced enormous growth in previous decades, growing to more than fourteen million people in the year 2010. This growth came mainly, but not exclusively, from within Turkey itself. This does not mean that it did not change the cuisine of the city since many migrants arrived at the capital from rural areas in Anatolia and Kurdistan, bringing their way of eating with them. Like Rott, Horky focuses on one specific dish: Midye Dolma, or stuffed mussels, sold by Kurdish street vendors all over the city. This example presents a type of dish actually coming from the city but being closely linked to a new arriving migrant group.

From the street food hotspot of Istanbul, we travel north to a country that is not usually associated with street food—Norway. Kine Ariela Hemli presents her article "Norway's Street Food on Wheels" which addresses the situation in her hometown of Oslo. There, street food is seen as something very foreign and is often associated with low quality and low standards of hygiene—prejudices that lead us back to Ovejero's concept of ethno-narcissistic cuisine. But there is also a growing counter-movement in the form of gourmet food trucks similar to the model existing in Sweden. These food trucks, in which some of the best chefs of the country prepare the dishes, challenge the prejudice towards street food and have revitalized the discussion of a mobile food in Norway.

Jin Wang, in his contribution on Taiwanese food titled "Sichuan-flavored Beef Noodle Soup in Taipei," brings insight into one very specific example of a street food dish representing the change of eating habits brought by migrants. Beef was a very uncommon dish before the arrival of Mainland-Chinese immigrants after the Chinese civil war (1927–50). With the introduction of beef eating, beef noodle soup became popular and is seen today as the national dish of Taiwan. This example shows how a specific type of food and its associated eating habits, brought by immigrants, turns into something seen as authentic and local within a few generations.

Finally, Emily Arthy takes us back in time to seventeenth century England, showing in her article, "Eating London's Street Food, 1603–1714," that street food is not a modern phenomenon. Street food is a part of urban life stretching beyond the present. London grew during this time, mainly fueled by migration, and like today, these immigrants brought their own dishes with them. Emily Arthy also tries to get a view on how class differences shaped the city and the cuisine of its inhabitants while interweaving contemporary historical events that influenced the food landscape in London, from the Civil War (1642–51) to the rise of the East India Company in the eighteenth century.

Street Food: A Mobile Concept
Martina Kaller, John Kear, and Markus Mayer

This book is directed to food studies scholars and aficionados of street food alike. Given the fact that the topic scarcely receives mention in food studies, the necessity of this book becomes obvious. The studies at hand address combinations of social, economic, political, ethnic, and religious aspects of street food in globalized cities. None of the topics are groundbreaking; rather, all of them represent solidified fields of research. With the addition of the spatial focus on streets in urban centers, however, we shed light on a scantily studied research question. The focus on the interrelation between global migration and the ubiquity of street food in global cities makes the articles of this volume unique. The authors share various social science backgrounds and an education in global studies and/or global history. Additionally, they lend to this project the geographic variety of their origins, which brings a more comprehensive view to the subject as a whole of many cases and contexts.

Food prepared, sold, and eaten on the street immediately engages the senses when visiting one of today's major cities. At first glance Taipei and London, Istanbul and Vienna or, Los Angeles and Tel Aviv might be seen as very heterogeneous places, but there are some characteristics that link all the world's global cities, among them a permanent flow of migration and its presence in daily food consumption.

Throughout history, migrations from rural sites to urban spaces have marked the creation and the growth of cities while long distance migrations connected civilizations on a global scale with those cities at the foci. Hence, immigration into the urban landscape reshaped cities, while the newcomers also brought with them diverse eating habits and food ingredients. On closer examination, street food is the most apparent and immediate expression of the presence of migrants in the public sphere. As a research focus within the larger topic of global migrations, this phenomenon provides insight into metropolises, and the mobility of foods and food-ways around the globe.

Estimates indicate that in today's hubs for immigration such as New York City, 98 percent of street food vendors are either from Bangladesh, Egypt, Mexico, Ecuador, China, or Afghanistan.[1] This figure correlates with the situation in 1925, when the U.S. Department of Agriculture counted around 31,000 street food sellers in New York City. Ninety percent of them hailed from a foreign country which, in 1927, led the Department of Public Markets to issue copies of rules and regulations in English, Yiddish, and Italian.[2]

In this book, our insights originate in the foundations of the humanities and social sciences. We lean on a pioneer of modern anthropology, Marcel Mauss, who concluded that eating is a total social phenomenon.[3] Thus, we are dealing with people and their eating habits, their food economies, and the social implications in the past and present with an emphasis on immigration to globalized cities.

Few publications available so far agree upon the fact that research on street food in cities calls for a commitment to inter-disciplinarity. Departing from the current treatment of food in social and medical science falls to the growing fields of global studies and global history which are characterized by interdisci-

---

1. Sean Basinski, "Hot Dogs, Hipsters, and Xenophobia: Immigrant Street Food Vendors in New York," *Social Research* 81 no. 2 (Summer 2014): 398.

2. Earl R. French, *Push Cart Markets in New York City: A Preliminary Report* (Washington DC: US Department of Agriculture, 1925), 3; Suzanne Wasserman, "The Good Old Days of Poverty: Merchants and the Battle Over Pushcart Peddling on the Lower East Side." *Business and Economic History* 27, no. 2 (1998): 330–39.

3. Marcel Mauss, *The Gift: Forms and Functions of Exchange in Archaic Societies* (London: Cohen & West, 1966), 76–77.

plinary and a multi-spatial perspective on global interactions, entanglements, and the building of institutions.[4]

Towards a Working Definition of Street Food

As our starting point, we embrace the definition of the Food and Agriculture Organization (FAO) of the United Nations: "Street foods are 'ready-to-eat' foods and beverages prepared and/or sold by vendors or hawkers especially in the streets and other similar places."[5] Within this general definition the locations, interactions, and different forms of consumption of street food remains debatable.

The most basic aspect here is location. Placing something in the streets has less to do with physical roads but instead points to operating within a public space. This excludes fast-food restaurants that have a claim of ownership over the property containing their operation. There is also an outdoor element that distances street food from an enclosed establishment. At the same time, the client's interaction with the vendor or hawker also excludes vending machines or automated installations that sell snacks and bottled drinks in highly frequented public spaces.

The label 'ready-to-eat' proscribes several characteristics to the consumption of street food: It can be immediately consumed and requires no additional culinary effort on the part of the buyer. This distinguishes street food from products sold at markets that, while occupying a public space, need an intermediate step before consumption. These three aspects —'ready-to-eat', sold in the context of personal interaction, and located in public places—

---

4. Jürgen Osterhammel and Niels P. Petersson, *Globalization: A Short History* (Princeton, NJ: Princeton University Press, 2005).
5. Food and Agriculture Organization of the United Nations, *Street Foods*, FAO Technical Meeting Report (Rome: FAO, 1997), http://www.fao.org/docrep/W4128T/W4128T00.HTM.

shape our understanding of street food and illustrate that the definition is less concerned with the edible product than the imagined categories which incorporate street food into a single entity.

The scholarly consensus admits that while street food is sold in the street, food sold in the street is not necessarily street food. To provide an account of street food in the urban context depends on various entangled factors: (1) in terms of transportation and distribution, an accelerating process of globalization within the logistics of urban food supply, (2) the ingredients themselves and their availability in new urban markets, and (3) the different types of preparing and cooking those ingredients which had, albeit slowly, changed their appearance in urban contexts over time. By looking at the foods themselves, scholars have not always distinguished between dishes prepared by the vendors and ready-made industrial products sold by hawkers in the streets. Under the current UN definition, an ice-cream vendor who uses a pushcart or a stationary pastry seller who operates from a stable stand in highly frequented food hot spots, such as bus stations, factory entrances, public beaches, parks, etc., can be considered as street food vendors; however, they only serve and do not partly or entirely prepare the food they sell. Such a food vendor, often a newcomer in town, might find this kind of food selling a part of an individual survival strategy and would not unfrequently operate as a subcontractor of a local franchise. The franchisee acts as a micro-capitalist in an environment of poverty and exploitation.[6] In contrast to these franchise structures, the street food business, as evidenced in this volume, is socially, economically, and culturally far more complex.

When observing the preparation of street food, the personal background of the vendor plays an important role. Immigrants in-

---

6. Mike Davis, *Planet of Slums* (London: Verso, 2007), 175–94. The same argument was already stressed by Saskia Sassen, *Cities in a World Economy* (Thousand Oaks, CA: Pine Forge Press, 2000).

volve most of the family in the preparation and commercialization of street food delicacies. Hence, kinship relations can be notable in the business organization. An example of a highly differentiated family business can be found in Mexico City with its approximately 25 million inhabitants. In such an urban sprawl, street vending, especially selling food in the street, is a noticeable characteristic of Mexico's capital. A delicacy often overlooked by outsiders is Cuitlacoche (corn smut) stuffed in tacos, quesadillas, and tamales. Cuitlacoche is a fungus, typically considered a blight, which is deliberately induced to young corncobs in maize fields throughout the countryside. Freshly harvested, it constitutes a tasty ingredient, higher in protein than uninfected corn. Only specific groups of immigrants to the city have access to it. Actually, among the few suppliers of this product to the city, extended families form networks to provide this ingredient. Harvesting and transporting the fungus is a delicate business, and so is its preparation, because it spoils quickly.[7] Hence, serving Cuitlacoche tacos is the domain of street food vendors who count on reliable supply chains and illustrates the importance of freshness in the context of street food quality.[8] This also has an effect on the consumer side, in that there must be an assumption of trust in the hawker's ability to offer a home-grown and freshly processed product that is technically a "ruined" crop. Diners in a restaurant setting would definitely not ask for Cuitlacoche, except at high priced tourist eateries, where costumers get a frozen product, which had lost its unique taste.

---

7. A. Martínez-Flores, J. J. Corrales-García, T. Espinosa-Solares, P. G. García-Gatica, C. Villanueva-Verduzco, "Cambios postcosecha del hongo comestible Cuitlacoche (Ustilago maydis (D. C.) Corda)," *Revista Chapingo Serie Horticultura* 14, no. 3, (2008): 340, http://www.scielo.org.mx/pdf/rcsh/v14n3/v14n3a16.pdf.

8. In the social sciences "freshness," like "taste," is a very questionable concept, which unfortunately cannot be discussed here. The introductory chapter by Susanne Freidberg. *Fresh: A perishable history*, (Cambridge, MA: Harvard University Press, 2009) gives insight into this multiplexity.

This combination of location, special dishes, and logistics, which would typify any restaurant, is also crucial to any street food business. If the owners are immigrants, they usually experience a tough process of conquering a space in the streets. The success stories frequently start with providing cheap and fresh foods for fellow immigrants. The subsequent decisions include offering locally recognized dishes alongside their home style cuisine. Frequently, this combined approach of meeting the demands of diverse customers leads to the creation of combinations of both of cuisines. With that said, street food vendors provide three economic functions: They are creative food retailers to mostly low-income consumers. They are operating in complex economic interactions, often including the family, marked by a clear spirit of entrepreneurship. Like any other street venders, only in exceptional cases are they linked to a so-called informal economy with ties to tax evasion and criminal organization. It would be equally valid to consider these street food vendors as "grassroots community entrepreneurs providing integral linkages to cities' economies."[9]

The authors of this volume agree on an additional phenomenological feature: city life in all its expressions simply cannot be imagined without street food. This includes its mode of production, its economic independence, and petty capitalists or self-employed entrepreneurs. They often operate in the face of informal and official obstructionism alike, and the demands of a diverse group of consumers. Elevated income prospects for individuals engaged in street food operations can be observed alongside exploitation. Organizational proscriptions dominate this economic environment in the form of government regulations, kinship relations, and mafia structures as well.

---

9. John Gaber, "Manhattan's 14th Street Vendor's Market: Informal Street Peddler's Complementary Relationship with New York City's Economy," *Urban Anthropology and Studies of Cultural Systems and World Economic Development* 23, no. 4 (1994): 401.

Also, street food consumers belong to different social, economic, and cultural groups. They include immigrants and commuters to the city—a group which encompasses most of the street food vendors themselves—as well as city folks who lack access to a minimal infrastructure for cooking such as construction and road workers who are often single men. But they are also confirmed by urban food adventures expressively loving exotic food. They publicly demonstrate their interest for new foods and simultaneously show their general acceptance of immigrants in town. This phenomenon, however, only describes a set of street food consumers in affluent societies. An observation from the larger metropolitan area of Accra, Ghana describes how street food is sold everywhere in the city, but people are rarely seen eating it on the streets. It is said that such a behavior could provoke jealousy where food is scarce or in societies where starvation and hunger are still in the collective memory of at least a part of the population. Not surprisingly, eating one's own portion without sharing it would be seen as problematic conduct. By considering prevailing communal cultural patterns, including conspicuous consumption, such a rationale appears highly coherent.[10]

From the perspective of the consumer, the omnipresence of street food in global cities constitutes an additional common feature which remains little noticed: it meets the needs of rich and poor customers alike. Business ghettos in inner cities and shantytowns share the obvious quality of lacking access to kitchens, stoves, fuel, and, on occasion, drinking water. Such very practical and obvious restrictions make street food consumption unavoidable across geographical and historical urban environments. Whether considered bad manners, as is visible in Old-Greek texts,

---

10. We owe this observation to the historian Silvia Ruschak-Schneider who undertook an extensive field research on textiles in Ghana. Silvia Theresia Antonia Ruschak, "Stoffe, die globale Geschichte machen" (PhD diss., University of Vienna, 2009).

or praised as a relaxing moment of personal interaction, as described in modern lifestyle magazines and food blogs, street food belongs to urbanity.[11] Eventually, the overall present changes of culturally rooted habits caused by migration also affect the consumption of food in urban environments. These changes are inherent to globalization processes faced by all social classes.

A Theoretical Framework

The essays at hand include discussions of street food in multiple historical and geographical contexts with a similar intent. They deconstruct the main signifiers "street" and "food" in the context of their scholarly discourses. That is not, however, the primary purpose of this introduction. Instead, each contribution in this volume negotiates the concept of street food and, where necessary, explores the boundaries of its components.

Inspired by Rosi Braidotti's theory of nomadic subjects, we can prove that the intercultural and transcultural nature of street food constitutes an outcome of migration.[12] Given this fact, it can be pointed out as a sign of "the rise of neo-nomadic cultures."[13] The emphasis on migration in this book highlights the flows of materials, persons, and ideas bound with street food.

Adam McKeown argues that globalizing migration encourages a more comprehensive examination of phenomena by logically linking different contexts together and encouraging new

---

11. Antonia-Leda Matalas and Mary Yannakoulia, "Greek Street Food Vending: An Old Habit Turned New," in *Street Foods*, eds. Artemis P. Simopoulos and Ramesh V. Bhat (Basel: Karger, 2000), 3.

12. Rosi Braidotti, *Nomadic Subjects: Embodiment and Sexual Difference in Contemporary Feminist Theory* (New York: Columbia University Press, 1994).

13. Marina Calloni, "Street Food on the Move: A Socio-philosophical Approach" *Journal of the Sciences of Food and Agriculture* 93, no. 14 (2013): 3406.

methodological approaches.[14] This correlates with Leslie Page Moch's depiction of migration as points of human contact and connection seen as a springboard to the *spatialization* of cuisine, culture, and identity.[15]

By choosing an urban-migration approach to the topic of street food in a global perspective, this volume occurs at a nexus of several theoretical strands. The most prominent are cultureal hybridization and glocalization. Both discourses address opposing and reciprocal interactions of proximate and extra-proximate developments in the process of globalization. In the course of the cultural turn, this homogenization-indigenization dynamic populated Appadurai's theory on hybridity in a global world.[16] He theorizes imaginary categories that define and distinguish collective identities in terms of customs and tradition. While hybridization has included space and otherness in its constructions, the approach to research on glocalization has brought geography to the forefront as a part of the spatial turn of the 1990s. In brief, glocalization describes the mutual permeability of global and local categories as an extension of the particular-universal divide.[17] Sociologist Roland Robertson popularized the concept in academic discourse as a response to the perception that globalization was a homogenizing process which supersedes locality.[18] He highlights the feedback and

---

14. Adam McKeown, "Global Migration, 1846–1940," *Journal of World History* 15, no. 2 (2004): 156, accessed January 27, 2014. doi: 10.1017/ S00208590060002859; and Adam McKeown, "Regionalizing World Migration," *International Review of Social History* 52 (2007): 134–35, doi: 10.1017/S00208590060002859.

15. Leslie Page Moch, "Connecting Migration and World History: Demographic Patterns, Family Systems and Gender," *International Review of Social History* 52 (2007): 97, doi: 10.1017/S002085900600280X.

16. Arjun Appadurai, *Modernity at Large: Cultural Dimensions of Globalization* (Minneapolis: University of Minnesota Press, 1996), 32.

17. Roland Robertson, "Globalisation or Glocalisation?" *Journal of International Communication* 18, no. 2 (2012): 196, doi: 10.1080/13216597.2012.709925.

18. Robaertson, "Globalisation or Glocalisation?" 192.

adaptation of norms evident in local and global spaces of thought and action. This again mirrors Appadurai's concept of "*dis-junctures*," imagining worlds that serve to intertwine the triumphantly universal and the resiliently particularity in the context of the deterritorialization of the nation-state.[19] Street food as a globally and locally constructed phenomenon interacts with both of these discourses in its tie to migration—to the flows of human beings and diverse mindsets to the particular habits they bring with them.

Regardless of which direction the pendulum will swing, social tensions frequently accompany migration. Such tensions might give rise to social creativity marked by the daily reinventing of urban life and, often in the same time and place, can be noticed as a conflict with local morals. Conservatives rather feel that the spread of multicultural street food stands over the city represents an aggression to local idiosyncrasies. Two articles of this book deal with this kind of rejection towards the way immigrating groups are reshaping foods and consumption patterns in global cities. Yet, advocates of street vending are no less squeamish in dooming the conservative voices in a generalized manner. For example, The Street Vendor Project in New York posted on January 25, 2016: "People who like Donald Trump don't like street vendors. Billionaire real estate developers do not like street vendors. Racists and xenophobes do not like street vendors. Arrogant, bombastic, narcissists do not usually like street vendors."[20] Both sides express arbitraty and one-sided interests. Therefore, dichotomous concepts tend to overshadow this complex, omnipresent phenomenon and its long lasting history in the development of cities. Whether they are defending so-called traditional street foods or oppose post-modern melting pots of tastes and habits, they operate in the same political climate, yet street food vendors are operating under ultimately disparate economic

---

19. Appadurai, *Modernity at Large*, 33.

20. "You're Fired!" The Street Food Project, January 25, 2016, last accessed June 30, 2016, http://streetvendor.org/youre-fired/.

and social conditions.[21] Street food hawkers can clearly be linked to any political group in town. No doubt, street food and political action merge only under very specific circumstances, as in the case of the Occupy Wallstreet movement.[22]

A final remark to theory goes to a common characteristic of street food eating. Street food consumers usually come from all social classes. Even though it is commonly stated that consuming street food means to act inside of a chaotic sphere of non-rules, eating at a street food stand is not free of etiquette.[23] Street food consumers also belong to a group defined by their behaviors of consumption. For example, if someone asks for a table napkin at a Döner Kebab stall, they will not only be considered ridiculous, but they also catapult themselves out of the peer group despite the fact that consuming beloved finger foods most likely ends with sauce on the eater's jacket. This observation evidently contradicts Norbert Elias' century-old thesis that civilization accompanies a decline in the threshold of embarrassment.[24]

State of Research

Admitting the omnipresence of street food in cities everywhere in the world, it is surprising that the topic plays little more

---

21. Kristina Graaff and Noa Ha, eds., *Street Vending in the Neoliberal City: A Global Perspective on the Practices and Policies of a Marginalized Economy* (New York: Bergham Books, 2015).
22. Maggie Dickinson, "Cooking up a Revolution: Food as a Democratic Tactic at Occupy Wall Street," *Food, Culture & Society: An International Journal of Multidisicplinary Research* 16, no.3 (2013).
23. Maren Möhring, *Fremdes Essen: Die Geschichte der ausländischen Gastronomie in der Bundesrepublik Deutschland* (Munich: Oldenbourg Verlag, 2012), 427. For more details, see Simon Reitmeier, *Warum wir mögen, was wir essen: Eine Studie zur Sozialisation der Ernährung* (Bielefeld: Transcript Verlag, 2013).
24. Norbert Elias, *The Civilizing Process* (New York: Urizen Books, 1978).

than a Cinderella role in food studies.[25] Two major approaches span the field: On the one hand, a culinary and tourist view focuses on the specific types of street food dishes as objects of study, often while providing recipes. Within this view, dishes and their presentation define the genre in culinary terms. With the alternative approach, the emphasis centers on the politics of food in the form of regulations, hygiene standards, and the access to cheap food for low class consumers with a strong emphasis on developing countries. The methods of production and regulation provide definition in a more top-down manner that is less concerned with specific contexts. These studies usually provide policy recommendations to governments.[26] Occasionally, they lack a notion for the historic condition of the phenomenon and are marked by an imprecise use of the term "informality."[27] Its omnipresence underlines that street food in cities constitutes a display of city life, both past and present. It is remarkable that supply-side foci remain often forgotten in food studies, which tend toward a preoccupation with dishes and the food itself. The allegedly questionable conditions of street food draw more attention than its matter of fact.

A strong tendency in existing publications on street food caters to the consumer curiosity of bringing home tastes and designs of dishes served in urban streets around the globe. Does preparing street food at home avoid the issues of social segregation

---

25. Alan Davidson, *The Oxford Companion to Food*, 2nd ed, ed. Tom Jaine. (Oxford: Oxford University Press, 2002), 759–60; Kenneth F. Kiple and Kriemhild Coneè Ornelas, eds., *The Cambridge World History of Food* (Cambridge: Cambridge University Press, 2000); and Jeffery M. Pilcher, *Food in World History* (New York: Routledge, 2006).

26. Benjamin Etzold, *The Politics of Street Food: Contested Governance and Vulnerabilities in Dhaka's Field of Street Vending* (Stuttgart: Franz Steiner Verlag, 2013).

27. Anthropologist and prominent food scholar Sidney W. Mintz mentions these arguments in his review of a book on street foods in Kingston. Sidney W. Mintz, review of *Street Foods of Kingston*, by Dorian Powell, Erna Brodber, Eleanor Wint, and Versada Campbell, *New West Indian Guide* 66, no.3–4 (1999): 315–16.

and hygiene? Does it remove the characterization as street food? Under the premises of this book, such questions remain open.

By conducting research on popular perceptions among book readers, there is little surprise that the culinary approach to street food overshadows academic research. While keeping in mind that serious academic books have only recently become a part of ordinary book commerce, large online retailers list about 400 books under the catchwords "street" plus "food"—all of which provide recipes and photographs. In other publications and food blogs, street food takes the appearance of haute cuisine. This leads to the artistic perception of the phenomenon, for instance, Joseph Carlson's illustrated book *Mobile food and foodhunting*.[28] Among this bunch of primarily a esthetic cookbooks there are two editions which supply more extensive information about the historical and environmental background of different street food. The practically oriented book *Street Foods* by Hinnerk von Bargen is more than anything else a textbook for inquiries into culinary science and commercial use of international flavors with origins in street foods.[29] The title edited by Bruce Kraig and Colleen Taylor Sen, on the other hand parts form the American experience of street food and extends to distant geographies in its description of local street food operations.[30] The book pairs this global bent with a range of color photographs and recipes. A book review published on Hollis Full Catalog captures this odd juxtaposition: "This encyclopedia is a bit of a misfire because it doesn't know what it wants to be—a travel guide or a cookbook."[31]

---

28. Joseph Carlson, *Mobile Food and Foodhunting* (Freiburg: Winwood 48 Edition, 2013).

29. Hinnerk von Bargen, *Street Foods* (John Wiley & Sons: Hoboken, 2016)

30. Bruce Kraig and Colleen Taylor Sen, eds., *Street Food around the World: An Encyclopedia of Food and Culture* (Santa Barbara: ABC, 2013).

31. Erin Linsenmeyer, review of *Street Food around the World: An Encyclopedia of Food and Culture*, eds. Bruce Kraig and Colleen Taylor Sen, *Booklist* 110, no. 9/10 (January 2014): 78, Academic Search Alumni Edition, EBSCOhost.

In addition to these recent volumes, a decade earlier the Oxford Symposium on Food and Cookery was dedicated to the topic "Public Eating." Its proceedings published in 1991 are characterized by a culinary acceptance and a curiosity for street food practices.[32] It does not rigidly align contributions along a common research focus but rather provides a varied tableau of specific regional cases marked by a wide range of research interests, not all of them being strictly academic.

If we consider academic street food publications, we find a stark contrast in both tone and content. Coincidentally, there exists a highly relevant new volume titled *Street Food: Culture, Economy, Health and Governance*, edited by Ryzia De Cássia Vieira Cardoso, Michèle Companion, and Stefano Roberto Marras.[33] The volume illustrates the immense diversity and economic and cultural significance of street food. It highlights the fact that street food matters particularly to poor or vulnerable groups of people, explicitly to women and immigrants. Brazilian nutritionists dominate the group of contributors to the volume. In a list of possible threat tourists may face when eating at a food stall in the Global South, it should not surprise that articles on governance and food safety in developing countries mark the trend of topics. Economic informality contributed to issues of food safety and quality in the form of pollen, dust, insects, the use of waste oil, and unsanitary housing combined with low levels of schooling—and hence, carelessness regarding hygiene. The onus for such worry is placed on the street food vendors. Does poverty not also mark the lives of street food consumers? No doubt they seek cheap foods, but this remains absent in the volume. The two articles highlighting

---

32. *Public Eating*, Proceedings of the Oxford Symposium on Food and Cookery (London: Prospect Books, 1992).
33. Ryzia De Cássia Vieira Cardoso, Michèle Companion, and Stefano Roberto Marras, eds., *Street Food: Culture, Economy, Health and Governance* (London: Routledge, 2014).

the role of women in the street food business provide confirmation oft-overlooked reality. Street food vendors usually earn above
minimum wage. This questions the assumption of considering
street food selling an informal economic activity. If revenues were
not calculable, such conclusions could not be drawn. The book
does provide anthropological and geographical insights to the
phenomenon and represents a successful attempt of academics
to give a comprehensive overview. They also include a holistic
approach to street food as championed by the UN World Health
Organization and the UN Food and Agriculture Organization.

Another volume, simply titled *Street Foods*, follows a similar direction in a more specialized way. *Street Foods* deals with
bio-medical research and its increasing influence on policy mak-
ers and public authorities who deal with street food in developing
countries.[34] Among the many technical articles, the contribution
of the volume addresses a historic topic: Street Food in ancient
and contemporary Greece. It matches the other contributions in-
sofar as the Ancient World experts of dietetics also disparaged
street food consumption for its unsanitary conditions. It goes
without saying that these ancient dietetics would focus on the
consumer's moral weakness when he or she dared to attend a
street food stand. Street food vending possessed the stigma of a
poor business, and it was considered inappropriate of Athens' po-
lis members. Although not explicitly mentioned, this article helps
to conceive how powerfully expert's admonitions influenced the
behavior of some individuals. At the same time, the large majority
of urban folks ignored such considerations and simply sought out
an easy, cheap, and warm dish.

The landscape of food study journal articles dealing with
street food is sparsely populated as are the findings of edited volumes and monographs. The international *Food History Bibliogra-*

---

34. Artemis V. Simopoulos and Ramesh V. Baht, *Street Foods, World Review of
Nutrition and Dietetics* 86 (Basel: Karger, 2000)

phy lists six entries: one in *Food & Foodways*, two in *Food, Culture, & Society: An International Journal of Multidisciplinary Research*, and three in *Gastronomica: The Journal of Food and Culture*.[35] The topics are street foods in Mexico City, food as a democratic tactic at Occupy Wall Street, Balut, a Philippines street food, women's resistance through street food vending in Haiti, Chicago's food trucks, and Turkish bread (simit) vending. Together with two articles in economics journals addressing the street hawking economy in general, which explicitly includes street food, the diversity of interests could not be larger, nor the attention to the topic in food studies poorer. This is also true of historical approaches to street food.

We are, in fact, not only what we eat, but also what our ancestors consumed.[36] Despite this, street-food has hardly found its way into explicit food history, much less when considered alongside immigration.[37] An exception is the recent book by B.W. Higman titled *How Food Made History*. Besides focusing on the later globalization waves in food history, he briefly mentions the

---

35. Dickinson, "Cooking up a Revolution"; Janet Long-Solís, "A Survey of Street Foods in Mexico City," *Food & Foodways* 15, no. 3–4 (2007): 213–36; Ty Matejowsky, "The Incredible, Edible *Bahlut*," *Food, Culture, & Society: An International Journal of Multidisciplinary Research* 16, no. 3 (September 2013): 387–404; Myron M. Beasley, "Women, *Sabotaj*, and Underground Food Economies in Haiti," *Gastronomica: The Journal of Critical Food Studies* 12, no. 2 (Summer 2012): 33–44; Geoff Dougherty, "Chicago's Food Trucks: Wrapped in Red Tape," *Gastronomica: The Journal of Critical Food Studies* 12, no. 1 (Spring 2012):62–65; and Alisa Roth, "Simit: Turkey's National Bread," *Gastronomica: The Journal of Critical Food Studies* 12, no. 4 (Winter 2012): 31–36.

36. Gary Nabhan, *Why Some Like it Hot: Food, Genes, and Cultural Diversity* (Washington D.C.: Island Press, 2004), 30, quoted in Linda Civitello, *Cuisine & Culture: A History of Food and People*, 3rd ed. (Hoboken, NJ: John Wiley & Sons, 2011), viii.

37. Donna R. Gabaccia, *We are What We Eat: Ethnic Food and the Making of the Americans*, (Cambridge, MA: Harvard University Press, 2000).

economic and social-historical aspects of street food. By 100 BC, ancient Rome was an urban agglomeration of more than one million inhabitants where "most of the city's people lived in tenements and had no access to the bulky ovens and hearths needed to bake bread or make porridges and gruels."[38] No wonder that common people were forced to purchase their ready-made food at outdoor sites where they also ate it.[39]

Street Food: Informal or Impoverished?

Street food also represents an opportunity to meet and socialize: the outdoor setting and the lack of set dining times facilitate interpersonal relations, be it at the Forum Romanum, an all-American hot dog stand, a colorful beef-noodles-booth in Taipei, a hawker's tray full of stuffed mussels in Istanbul, the Viennese Würstelstand, or a taco stall in Los Angeles. Yet, does street food actually represent a cheap option for poor eaters? Obviously, this question deserves more attention.

One approach for studying the historical development of the phenomenon is linking street food to military provision. Recently, high-fashioned food trucks remind us of this logistically driven relationship. Chosen by Martina Kaller as a crucial approach to all convenient foods, so far this obvious connection to street food is only explicitly shared by food historian Lynn Olver.[40] In the introduction to her electronic food-timeline library

---

38. B.W. Higman, *How Food Made History* (Chichester, West Sussex: Wiley-Blackwell, 2012), 151.

39. A sign of the limited in-depth research on the topic is the fact that years before Higman, Linda Civitello mentioned the same example in History of Food and People. Linda Civitello, *Cuisine & Culture: A History of Food and People*, 3rd ed. (Hoboken, NJ: John Wiley & Sons, 2011), 52.

40. Martina Kaller, *Essen unterwegs: Eine kleine Globalgeschichte von Mobilität und Wandel am Teller* (Linz: Oberösterreichische Landesmuseen, 2011).

she dedicates one subchapter to street food stating: "The history of mobile street vending (in the broadest sense) can be traced to military field mess units. The idea of cooking and serving food from portable canteens evolved over time."[41] With an eye to the nineteenth and early twentieth century theaters of war in Europe and East Asia, the serving of food on the road, at the battle front or supplying civilians en masse following invasion and the destruction of infrastructure established street food as a necessity for thousands and more. As cities in Germany and Japan suffered complete destruction at the end of World War II street food also became ingrained in the collective memory of survival and postwar reconstruction.[42] The focus here does not lie either in the calorie intake per person or nutritional balance. What mattered for the war survivors was having access to one warm meal a day in the economic and political uncertainty of postwarcircumstances. This illustrates an essential function of street food. Research on medieval society records monks and nuns who placed soup kitchens on the streets to feed the poor. In the nineteenth century the British philanthropic movements did the same in the city of London.

As sociologist and philosopher Marina Calloni points out, street food in the period of industrialization served to differentiate social classes.In the age of globalization, however, it is linked to diverse ethnic groups and their presence in megacities. To Calloni, the most historically characteristic street food of the age of industrialization is "Fish and Chips." She points our that in nineteenth century Britain,

---

41. Lynne Olver, "Street Food," in *The Food Timeline Online* (2000), last modified January 16, 2015, http://www.foodtimeline.org/restaurants.html#streetfood.

42. Philip Jinseop Lee, "Instant Ramen as Forrest Gump: Postware Japan in Food" (honors thesis, Wesleyan University, 2015), 7.

"the necessity to eat quickly in order to return to work, to earn more money together with the impossibility of living in suitable housing in which to prepare proper meals, included new industrial workers, [who] settled in unfriendly urban environments... This led to the enormous success of 'fish and chips' (apparently imported by Portuguese Sephardic Jews of the diaspora)."[43]

Re-examining this view as a particular feature of street food in the context of industrial growth, Calloni also mentions the badly reputed food for the poor and needy—an assessment acquired from its supposedly unhealthy, and above all low cost characteristics. This view also explains why concerns about street food and regulations of its sale became a topic of regulation and is currently the purview of development studies. A bourgeois design of properly eating assumes that healthy and safe food is eaten indoors at the family table. No doubt, this is an idealized image and likely reflects notions of tradition and archaic fears of food intake alike.[44]

Calloni's observation finds confirmation in social science journal articles since the early 1980s. They mainly point out the dangers inherent in the consumption of street food. Quite few of them deal with socio-economic factors: Irene Tinker's pivotal works of the 1980s and 1990s reflect upon poverty conditions in global societies. She has written on street food from the perspective of economic micro-enterprise and empowerment for women, and, not surprisingly, finds fault with the mainstream perspective of the Western model:

"Generalizations about women's domestic roles based on U.S. and European models resulted in inappropriate programs and ethno-

---

43. Marina Calloni, "Street Food on the Move," 3407.
44. Martina Kaller, *Macht über Mägen: Essen machen statt Knappheit verwalten. Haushalten in einem Mexikanischen Dorf* (Vienna: Promedia, 2002.

centric theories. Urban planning… [initiatives in development countries tried] to impose unattainable standards on sellers of street foods."[45]

In assuming Calloni's stance on "reinterpreting of traditions in a globalized world",[46] we must recognize that most street food preparers and, depending the cultural setting, street food vendors in the globalized world are female. As a matter of fact, regulation of the street food sector negatively affects women in the majority of instances. For the case of Los Angeles Fazila Bhimji highlights identity and sense of belonging among women street food vendors in Los Angeles.[47] This oft unseen aspect of making a living in a globalized world deserves further research.

Migration of Taste

By exploring the overlap between the notions of ethnic food and street food, we enrichen our understanding of how street food interacts in context. Cities have always allowed for quicker assimilation than rural areas and small towns due to the increased proximity and anonymity of urban spaces. Large cities also pro-

45. Irene Tinker, "Street Foods: Traditional Microenterprise in a Modernizing World," *International Journal of Politics, Culture and Society* 16, no. 3 (Spring 2003): 331–49. http://www.jstor.org/stable/20020170.
46. Calloni. "Street Food on the Move," 3011. "It was the railway, followed by the use of ice and steam trawling, that revolutionized the habits of fish consumption in this country [England], and converted fish from something in the nature of an expensive food into a food of the working class." Charles Latham Cuting, *Fish Saving: A History of Fish Processing from Ancient to Modern Times* (London: Leonard Hill, 1955), 217, quoted in Panikos Panayi, *Fish and Chips: A History* (London: Reaktion Books, 2014), 22.
47. Fazila Bhimji, "Struggles, Urban Citizenship, and Belonging: The Experience of Undocumented Street Vendors and Food Truck Owners in Los Angeles," *Urban Anthropology and Studies of Cultural Systems and World Economic Development* 39, no. 4 (Winter 2010): 455–92, http://www.jstor.org/stable/41291334.

vided markets for food vendors, from humble pushcarts to the legendary hot dog stalls in Coney Island. American food-ways are particularly marked by ethnicity—namely the results of theimmigration wave of 1880–1924. In an article about the succession of ethnic foods becoming genuine to American society, food historian Jeffrey Pilcher asks: "How long does it take for food to become naturalized, or, to use the language of American nationalism and immigration history, to become 'old stock'?"[48] He comes to the conclusion, apart from most European scholars of the field, that in America "the process of naturalization has taken place between multiple ethnic groups rather than as a confrontation between foreign foods and a monolithic mainstream".[49] This dynamic is not restricted to the New World. There is also a clear tension between the familiar and the new in the urban culinary landscape.

Most foreign street food habits were not immediately welcomed in the towns of continental Europe and often had been, and still are, seen as a threat to local street foods. In Germany, the street food Döner Kebab has often been discussed with retention. Postwar Germans were willing to adapt the venerable sausage to the logistical reality but showed less flexibility in adopting unfamiliar street foods, especially when those foods accompanied mainly poor immigrants from Turkey. At Döner Kebab stands Turkish immigrants fused the Döner, roasted meat on a spit which was a formerly festive dish, with Kebab, a type of bun called *tombik pide*, and sold it according to what was expected by the population at an *Imbissstube*.[50] While Döner Kebab has become a popular, cheap lunch option for everyone's wallet, there remain tensions surrounding the vendors preparing Döner Ke-

---

48. Jeffrey M. Pilcher, "'Old stock' Tamales and Migrant Tacos: Authenticity and Naturalization of Mexican Food" *Social Research: An International Quarterly* 81, no. 2 (Summer 2014): 441, DOI: 10.1353/sor.2014.0018.
49. Pilcher, "'Old stock' Tamales and Migrant Tacos," 460.
50. Peter Heine, *Food Culture in the Near East, Middle East, and North Africa* (Westpot, CT: Greenwood Publishing Group, 2004); and Maren Möhring, *Fremdes Essen*, 422–32.

bab in public spaces. Since the mid-1970s, Turkish Kebab-stands have popped up at numerous street corners in cities of Western Germany without replacing the local *Currywurst*.[51] The latter is so popular that it is hardly known that it was invented only after World War II due to food shortages. This reminds us of the fact that almost all products served as ready-made food originate in war, or the scarcity of their aftermath They meet the need of a cheap, permanent food supply. However, the Currywurst has become a synonym for characteristic German street food.[52] It quite reproduces the "myth of eating *Heimat* properly," which should not be confused with the trend of "locavorism" (the preference of buying agricultural products from local growers). The term "Heimat" adds the notion of the place of origin of a person which, in the German language, makes it an emotionally loaded term.[53]

Something quite similar to the invention of the Currywurst tradition in Germany happened decades before with hot dogs in the United States. Bruce Kraig coherently describes its history, going into detail about its presumed invention in the 1860s by a German immigrant to New York. This unnamed person likely sold Wieners inside of rolls topped with Sauerkraut.[54] The naming of "hot dogs" first appeared in a school magazine at Yale University, issued in 1895.[55] Market leaders like Nathan's Hot Dogs claim the invention of hot dogs for themselves, and they also nourish myths of immigrants' success stories. In celebrating the founder of this hot dog company on the website, it is mentioned that also the hot dog

---

51. Möhring, *Fremdes Essen*, 120.

52. Deutsches Currywurst Museum Berlin Website, www.currywurstmuseum. com, accessed January 20, 2015.

53. Martina Kaller, "Wider die heimat-verkorkste Richtig-Tuerei beim Essen," in *Esskulturen. Gutes Essen in Zeiten mobiler Zutaten*, eds. Andrea Heistinger and Daniela Ingruber (Vienna: Mandelbaum, 2010), 102–19.

54. Bruce Kraig, *Hot Dog: A Global History* (Chicago: University of Chicago Press, 2009).

55. *The Yale Record*, May 1, 1895, quoted in Kraig, *Hot Dog: A Global History*, 127.

history roots in immigration: "Polish immigrant, Nathan Handwerker… started his business in 1916 in the streets of Coney Island, New York", where he sold hot dogs "manufactured based on a recipe developed by his wife, Ida."[56] Unfortunately for this version, evidence about the success of hot dogs exists before 1916. Hot dogs met massive crowds at Chicago's World's Fair in 1893. Thousands of visitors experienced them. Reliable records on hot dogs also link its creation to immigrant influence, both in terms of the sausage itself and the way of serving it as finger-food inside of a roll with mustard on top. At the archive of the History Museum of Chicago, records prove that Emil Reichel, emigrant of Vienna, and Sam Ladany, immigrant to Chicago from Prague, both of them butchers, started their beef business in 1894 and surprisingly became trend-setters.[57] They introduced and popularized hot dogs as a later indispensable street food in America. According to the founder's dietary restrictions, the original hot dog sausage was kosher.[58]

The same happened to the street food par excellence: pizza. With slices sold in every street corner of this globalized world, impressive marketing efforts continually undertake the dissimulation of its multiple proveniences in every wheat-based civilization. The name finds roots in the Italian, more specifically Neapolitan, language of nineteenth century. At the end of the same century, pizza making was transferred to the United States together with immigrants from Italy escaping hunger. Here ends the Italian part of the pizza's history, as the dish took on an American flavor. It would eventually spawn an entire food industry. Pizza experienced a massive industrialization and found its way into fast food chains. It did not take long until the slice of bread

---

56. "Nathan's Famous History," Nathan's Famous Website, 2015, http://nathansfamous.com/story/extended_history.

57. "Vienna Beef Company History Timeline," Vienna Beef Website, 2015, http://www.viennabeef.com/our-company.

58. For more details see Kaller, *Essen unterwegs*, 80–96.

topped with leftovers found its way into households of all social classes—a convenient food, ordered from home-delivery services, and available as a ready-made frozen dish. At the same time as it became native to America, it started to be commercialized as a world-conquering street food, and an expression of pop culture.[59] Its successful spread was connected to the so called "Americanization" after World War II. The Cold War division of the world into two incompatible spheres of influence exemplifies the mental connection between food and people—the ideological conflict reflected in the lack of pizza in the Soviet Union.

Returning to the notion of Americanization of culture, this process was distrustfully described as cultural invasion—a repetitive stereotype applied to any influence from foreigners and their assumingly strange habits. This type of othering correlates with Pier Bourdieu's concept of distinction and remains one of the strongest markers of pro and contra arguments in the global scene of street food-ways in the urban space. Whether drawing upon this explanation or Pilcher's conclusion that new foods in town became "old stock" when new immigrants conquered the food market, the big picture encompassing the many different food ways in town remains elusive. Only closer scrutiny of the details and differences of the historical and the global phenomenon will allow for deeper insight into the phenomenon of street food in what we have come to call a globalized world.

---

59. Martina Kaller, "Die Erfindung von 'Pizza & Pasta': Italienisches Essen und italienische Einwanderung in den USA im 19. und 20. Jahrhundert," in *Kulinarishe "Heimat" und "Fremde": Migration und Ernährung im 19. Und 20. Jahrhundert*, eds. Lars Amenda and Ernst Langthaler, Jahrbuch für Geschichte des ländlichen Raumes 10 (Fall 2013), 54–71.

Bibliography

Amenda, Lars and Ernst Langthaler, eds. *Kulinarische "Heimat" und "Fremde": Migration und Ernährung im 19. und 20. Jahrhundert.* Jahrbuch für Geschichte des ländlichen Raumes 10. Innsbruck: Studienverlag, 2014.

Appadurai, Arjun. *Modernity at Large: Cultural Dimensions of Globalization.* Minneapolis: University of Minnesota Press, 1996.

Von Bargen, Hinnerk. *Street Foods.* Hoboken, NJ: John Wiley & Sons, 2016.

Basinski, Sean. "Hot Dogs, Hipsters, and Xenophobia: Immigrant Street Food Vendors in New York." *Social Research* 81, no. 2 (Summer 2014):397–408.

Bhimji, Fazila. "Struggles, Urban Citizenship, and Belonging: The Experience of Undocumented Street Vendors and Food Truck Owners in Los Angeles." *Urban Anthropology and Studies of Cultural Systems and World Economic Development* 39, no. 4 (Winter 2010): 455–92. http://www.jstor.org/stable/41291334.

Braidotti, Rosi. *Nomadic Subjects: Embodiment and Sexual Difference in Contemporary Feminist Theory.* New York: Columbia University Press, 1994.

Calloni, Marina. "Street Food on the Move: A Socio-philosophical Approach." *Journal of the Science of Food and Agriculture* 93, no. 14 (2013): 3406–13.

Cardoso, Ryzia De Cássia Vieria, Michèle Campnaion, and Stefano Roberto Marras, eds. *Street Food: Culture, Economy, Health and Governance,* London: Routledge, 2014.

Carlon, Joseph. *Mobile Food and Foodhunting.* Freiburg: Winwood48 Edition, 2013.

Civitello, Linda. *Cuisine and Culture: A History of Food and People.* 3rd ed. Hoboken, NJ: John Wiley & Sons, 2011.

Crenn, Chantal, Jean Pierre Hassoun, and Xavier Medina. "Migrations, pratiques alimentaire et rapports sociaux: Quand continuité n'est pas reproduction, discontinuity n'est pas rupture." *Anthropology of Food* 7 (December 2010). http://aof.revues.org/6515.

Davidson, Alan. *The Oxford Companion to Food.* 2nd ed. Edited by Tom Jaine. Oxford: Oxford University Press, 2002.

Davis, Mike. *Planet of Slums.* London: Verso, 2007.

Dickinson, Maggie. "Cooking up a Revolution: Food as a Democratic Tactic at Occupy Wall Street." *Food, Culture & Society: An International Journal of Multidisciplinary Research* 16, no. 3 (2013): 359–65

Diner, Hasia R. *Hungering for America: Italian, Irish, and Jewish Foodways in the Age of Migration.* Cambridge, MA: Harvard University Press, 2001.

Elias, Norbert. *The Civilizing Process.* New York: Urizen Books, 1978.

Etzold, Benjamin. *The politics of Street Food: Contested Governance and Vulnerabiliteis in Dhaka's Field of Street Vending.* Stuttgart: Franz Steiner Verlag, 2013.

Food and Agriculture Organization of the United Nations. *Street Foods.* FAO Technical Meeting Report. Rome: FAO, 1997. Accessed December 1, 2014. http://www.fao.org/docrep/W4128T/W4128T00. HTM.

———. "Ensuring Quality and Safety of Street Foods." *Food for the Cities Factsheets.* (Rome: FAO, 2009) Accessed October 28, 2014. ftp://ftp.fao.org/docrep/fao/011/ak003e/ak003e09.pdf.

Freidberg, Susanne. *Fresh: A Perishable History.* Cambridge, MA: Harvard University Press, 2009.

French, Earl R. *Push Cart Markets in New York City: A Preliminary Report.* Washington DC: US Department of Agriculture, 1925.

Gabaccia, Donna R., *We are What We Eat: Ethnic Food and the Making of Americans.* Cambridge, MA: Harvard University Press, 2000.

Gaber, John. "Manhattan's 14th Street Vendor's Market: Informal Street

Peddler's Complementary Relationship with New York City's Economy." *Urban Anthropology and Studies of Cultural Systems and World Economic Development* 23, no. 4 (1994): 373–408.

Graaff, Kristina, and Noa Ha, eds. *Street Vending in the Neoliberal City: A Global Perspective on the Practice and Policies of a Marginalized Economy.* New York: Bergham Books, 2015.

Heine, Peter. *Food Culture in the Near East, Middle East, and North Africa.* Westpot, CT: Greenwood Publishing Group, 2004.

Higman, B.W. *How Food Made History.* Chichester, West Sussex: Wiley-Blackwell, 2012.

Kaller, Martina. "Die Erfindung von 'Pizza & Pasta': Italienisches Essen und italienische Einwanderung in den USA im 19. Und 20. Jahrhundert." In *Kulinarische " Heimat" und "Fremde": Migration und Ernährung im 19. Und 20. Jahrhundert,* edited by Las Amenda and Ernst Langthaler, 54–71. Jahrbuch für Geschichte des ländlichen Raumes 10 (Fall 2013).

———. *Essen unterwegs: Eine kleine Globalgeschichte von Mobilität und Wandel am Teller.* Weitra: Verlag Bibliothek der Provinz, 2011.

———. *Macht über Mägen: Essen machen statt Knappheit verwalten. Hasuhalten in einem mexikanishen Dorf.* Vienna: Promedia, 2002.

———. "Wider die heimat-verkorkste Richtig Tuerei beim Essen." In *Esskulturen: Gutes Essen in Zeiten mobiler Zutaten.* Edited by Andrea Heistinger and Daniela Ingruber. Vienna: Mandelbaum, 2010.

Kelly, Alison P. "Food Writing: A Short Guide to Selected Resources." In *Science Reference Guides,* Library of Congress Science Reference Services. October 2007. http://www.loc.gov/rr/scitech/SciRefGuides/foodwriting.html.

Kiple, Kenneth F., and Kriemhild Coneè Ornelas, eds. *The Cambridge World History of Food.* Cambridge: Cambridge University Press, 2000.

Kraig, Bruce. *Hot Dog: A Global History.* Chicago: University of Chicago Press, 2009.

Kraig, Bruce, and Colleen Taylor Sen, eds. *Street Food around the World: An Encyclopedia of Food and Culture.* Santa Barbara: ABC, 2013.

Linsenmeyer, Erin. Review of *Street Food around the World: An Encyclopedia of Food and Culture,* edited by Bruce Kraig and Colleen Taylor Sen. *Booklist* 110, no. 9/10 (January 2014): 78. Academic Search Alumni Edition, EBSCOhost.#

Lee, Philip Jinseop. "Instant Ramen as Forrest Gump: Postware Japan in Food." Honor's Thesis, Wesleyan University, 2015.

Martínez-Flores, A., J.J. Corrales-García, T. Espinosa-Solares, P.G. Garcia-Gatica, and C. Villenueva-Verduzco. "Cambios postcosecha del hongo comestible huitlacoche (Ustilago maydis (D.C.) Corda)." *Revista Chapingo Serie Horticultura* 14, no. 3 (2008): 339–46.

Matalas, Antonia-Leda, and Mary Yannakoulia. "Greek Street Food Vending: An Old Habit Turned New." In *Street Foods,* edited by Artemis P. Simonpoulos and Ramesh V. Baht, 1–24. Basel: Karger, 2000.

Mauss, Marcel. *The Gift: Forms and Functions of Exchange in Archaic Societies.* London: Cohen & West, 1966.

McKeown, Adam. "Global Migration, 1846–1940." *Journal of World History* 15, no. 2 (2004). doi: 10.1353/jwh.2004.0026

———. "Regionalizing World Migration." *International Review of Social History* 52 (2007): 134–42. doi: 10.1017/S0020859006002859.

Mintz, Simon W. Review of *Street Foods of Kingston,* by Dorian Powell, Erna Brodber, Eleanor Wint, and Versada Campbell. *New West Indian Guide* 66, no. 3–4 (1999): 315–16.

Moch, Leslie Page. "Connecting Migration and World History: Demographic Patterns, Family Systems and Gender." *International Review of Social History* 52 (2007): 97–104. doi: 10.1017/S002085900600280X.

Möhring, Maren. *Fremdes Essen: Die Geschichte der ausländischen Gastronomie in der Bundesrepublik Deutschland.* Munich, Oldenbourg Verlag, 2012.

Olver, Lynne. "Street Food." In *The Food Timeline Online*. 2000, Last Modified January 16, 2015. http://www.foodtimeline.org/restaurants.html#streetfood.

Osterhammel, Jürgen, and Niels P. Petersson. *Globalization: A Short History*. Princeton, NJ: Princeton University Press, 2005.

Pilcher, Jeffery M., *Food in World History*. New York: Routledge, 2006.

———, "'Old Stock' Tamales and Migrant Tocos: Authenticity and Naturalization of Mexican Food." *Social Research: an International Quarterly* 81, no.2 (Summer 2014): 440–460.

Public Eating. Proceedings of the Oxford Symposium on Food and Cookery. London: Prospect Books, 1992.

Reitmeier, Simon. *Warum wir mögen, was wir essen: Eine Studie zur Sozialsation der Ernährung*. Bielefeld: Transcript Verlag, 2013.

Robertson, Roland. "Globalisation or Glocalisation?" *Journal of International Communication* 18, no. 2 (2012): 191-208. doi: 10.1080/13216597.2012.709925.

Ruschak, Silvia Theresia Antonia. "Stoffe, die globale Geschichte machen." PhD diss., University of Vienna, 2009.

Sassen, Saskia. *Cities in a World Economy*. Thousand Oaks, CA: Pine Forge Press, 2000.

Simopoulos, Artemis V., and Ramesh V. Baht. *Street Foods*. World Review of Nutrition and Dietetics 86. Basel: Karger, 2000.

Tinker, Irene. "Street Foods: Traditional Microenterprise in a Modernizing World." *International Journal of Politics, Culture and Society* 16, no. 3 (Spring 2003): 331–49. http://www.jstor.org/stable/2002017.

Wasserman, Suzanne. "The Good Old Days of Poverty: Merchants and the Battle over Pushcart Peddling on the Lower East Side." *Business and Economic History* 27, no. 2 (1998): 330–39.

Stirring the Melting Pot:
Ethno-narcissistic Cuisine and Surging Immigration in Contemporary Spain

Iván Ovejero

An Ethnic Marker with an Ethnographic Problem

What do we understand by "ethnic marker"? Ethnographers provide one simple, straightforward, and unequivocal answer: it depends on who you ask. In an attempt at a handy definition, we follow a school of constructivists who understand ethnic markers as anything that substantiates the belief in a shared ethnicity, i.e. a common culture and a common ancestry[1]. Much like how personal traits are lines—defining features—in the continuity of experience that constitutes individuality, ethnic markers are lines in the commonality of experience that constitutes ethnicity.

One of these lines is cuisine, with cooking becoming a proxy for ethnicity.[2] Precisely because we tend to eat in the company of others,[3] we observe written and unwritten regulations that standardize not only what, but also where, when, how, and to an extent even why we eat. Standards like these, beyond their civilizing purposes, can codify a commonality, a shared sense of belonging to a specific somewhere as opposed to a specific elsewhere. Most evident are these standards in: (1) the selection of ingredients, dictated as much by traditional prescriptions on what is edible as by logistic considerations on what is available; (2) the cooking proce-

---

1. Andreas Wimmer, "The Making and Unmaking of Ethnic Boundaries," *American Journal of Sociology* 113 (2008): 973.
2. Pierre L. van den Berghe, "Ethnic Cuisine: Culture in Nature," *Ethnic and Racial Studies* 7 (1984): 387.
3. The English word "company" is derived from the Latin *com* ("together") and *panis* ("bread").

dure, with the recurrence of certain kinds of heating and seasoning as patterns in a culinary theme; and (3) the act of eating itself, where norms cover anything from the order and timing of meals to general etiquette and ritualistic conventions. Cuisine is thus, like any other ethnic marker, a line by which inclusion defines itself against exclusion. And fiercely so, as cuisine is said to be one of most reliable ethnic markers, with culinary practices resisting forces as compelling as colonization, modernization, and urbanization.[4] It is perhaps this reliability that justifies our intuition that cuisine is reflective of the nature of ethno-national groups, as with "robust" English food or "aesthetic" Japanese dishes.

This reliability, however, seems unreliable. Culinary practices are usually less original and less consistent than intuitively assumed: Spaniards might not be pleased to be reminded that, until historically recently, tomatoes, potatoes, oranges, corn, cod, and spinach were not considered their traditional staples, or that today's Andalusians might feel like foreigners at a Catalonian table, while Austrians and Argentines may be unaware that, for some of their dishes, the most substantive difference is in the title at the top of the recipe.[5] Only through comparison can we ascertain difference and only with difference can inclusion define itself against exclusion. But if this difference seems blurrier than we expected, if our ethnic marker seems to be running out of ink, then it follows that, for the purpose of reliable representation, we cannot justify exclusion with traditional difference alone. Hence the need for artificial difference: that is, the result of an effort to fabricate representability, by which we mean an effort to exaggerate the importance of one's most exceptional attributes (e.g., a nation's basket of selected regional foods) to facilitate our opposition to, and thus our exclusion from, those who we wish to perceive, or to be perceived, as different from us.

---

4. Esther M. Rebato-Ochoa, "Las nuevas culturas alimentarias: Globalización vs. etnicidad," *Osasunaz* 10 (2009): 139.
5. Rebato-Ochoa, "Nuevas culturas alimentarias," 138.

Excessive nationalism is one way of conceiving artificial difference; ethno-narcissism, our ethnic variant for collective narcissism, could be another. It would probably take an eternity for psychoanalytic giants like Kernberg, Kohut, Freud, and Fromm to agree on the very essence of narcissism in a hypothetical faculty lounge, but we concentrate here on a fairly uncontroversial narcissistic trait: the need to self-identify.[6] A narcissistic self-identity consists of a series of pretenses or fabricated self-concepts, eventually undetectable as such, that are upheld as a misleadingly realistic representation of the self before others, a concept where the maxim of "being true to oneself" has been recast as "being falsely true to others."[7] Narcissists invent and perpetuate this false identity, firstly, because it enables them to assert themselves among others, even in the absence of established facts or actual behavior.[8] This identity, secondly, also serves to defend them from reality, which would otherwise make reminders of their unremarkability all the more unbearable. And thirdly, narcissists edit their identity, both highlighting and concealing parts of it, so as to reduce their full, bewildering complexity into a readily recognizable character, not only to assert and defend themselves, but also to ease the process of relating to others.

Now, if we climb up from the individual to the collective level, we can find psychoanalysts embedding aspects of this trait into the notion of "large-group identity," the subjective experience of thousands or millions of people bound by a persistent sense of sameness, whether religious or ethno-national, that is partly based

---

6. For the American Psychiatric Association, the diagnostic criteria for the narcissistic personality disorder include qualities as disparate as feelings of grandiosity, excessive envy, a fondness for power fantasies, an inability to empathize, and a proclivity to be interpersonally exploitative, among multiple others.

7. Andrew D. Brown, "Narcissism, Identity and Legitimacy," *Academy of Management Review* 22 (1997): 649.

8. Steven J. Bartlett, "Narcissism and Philosophy," *Methodology and Science* 19 (1986): 19.

on the multiple projections with which this collective defines itself against another.[9] We thus reason that ethno-national groups, knowing that their full diversity is unrepresentable in the world at large, knowing also that it is unrepresentable because most of it is unrecognizable, and knowing finally that it is unrecognizable because most of it is unremarkable, can operate as the narcissistic individual does: by molding their features into a useful artificial identity, which by logic defeats the purpose of reliable representation. Ethno-narcissism, therefore, should inform our understanding of cuisine as an ethnic marker.

An Ethno-national Group under a Multi-ethnic Influx

Should it indeed inform our understanding? This essay attempts to winnow the factual wheat from the theoretical chaff, to winnow behavior from identity, in the interest of establishing whether, and to what extent, ethno-narcissism could render new insights into the partial artificiality of cuisine as an ethnic marker. What is the nature of this artificiality? Can a partly artificial ethnic marker be swayed by a sweeping disruption? How does the cuisine of an ethno-national group respond to the introduction of culinary practices via mass immigration in one particular instance?

This instance is promising. Spain, a nation-state continually concerned with its ethno-national identity, absorbed a surge in immigration in the first decade after the turn of the century. As the OECD member that received the second highest number of immigrants in such period, this country saw a spectacular rise of the number of foreigners residing on its soil, with 900,000 in 2000 and 5.7 million in 2010, which translates to an increase from 2.2 percent to 12.2 percent in the share of foreigners

---

9. Vamik D. Volkan, "Transgenerational Transmissions and Chosen Traumas: An Aspect of Large-Group Identity," *Group Analysis* 34 (2001): 81.

relative to Spain's total population.[10] Within ten years, this ethno-national group, defined frequently (albeit not uncontroversially) as one with little extra-Iberian immigration since the 1980s, found itself exposed to a surging influx of immigrants who, on average: (a) hailed from Central and South America, North Africa, or Eastern Europe; (b) were young or middle-aged; (c) had a secondary education, with minorities either holding a university degree, or having little formal education; (d) were employed to a significant extent, notably those from Eastern Europe; and (e) reported to be overwhelmingly willing to stay in Spain over the longer term.[11] Considering this degree of integration, we assume that, if immigration can disrupt ethno-national cuisine and test the resilience of its artificiality, then modern Spain offers ideal conditions to measure this interaction. And especially so given Spain's stringent street food regulations, which restricted ethnic food sales to the formal economy, thus quantifying much of what transpired, and also given Spain's unusual wealth of official documentation on the culinary practices of the newly arrived. We thus explore this interaction, by means of simple statistical observations, within two areas of measurement: ethnic food consumption and national eating habits.

---

10. Joaquín Arango, *Exceptional in Europe? Spain's Experience with Immigration and Integration* (Washington, DC: Migration Policy Institute, 2013), 2; for the relevant legalese on who counts as an immigrant in Spain, see: Ley Orgánica 4/2000. Even if the official number of immigrants has varied as a result of the three amendments of this law, such variation does not invalidate the sheer magnitude of Spain-bound immigration since 2000.

11. Carmen González-Enriquez, "Spain," in *European Immigration: A Sourcebook*, ed. Anna Triandafyllidou and Ruby Gropas (Aldershot: Ashgate Publishing Limited, 2007), 331; Spanish Ministry of Agriculture, Fishing, and Food and Nielsen Corporation, *Hábitos alimentarios de los inmigrantes en España* (Madrid: Fotocomposición SA, 2007), 29–33; and Ignacio Lauroba and Carmen Ramos-Valverde, "Hábitos alimentarios de los inmigrantes en España," *Investigación y Marketing* 89 (2005): 43–45.

Adopting Migratory Tastes via Ethnic Food Consumption

A wry statistical quip reminds us that, while it is easy to lie with statistics, it is much easier to lie without them. We follow the less cynical version: while it is possible to lie with statistics, it is impossible to tell the truth without them. And this is particularly true if the data is both abundant and consistent, as with Spain's ethnic food consumption. Data trends are at best a revealing sign in a world of imperfect information. Whether compiled by public agencies or market-intelligence providers, studies, reports, and surveys provide a smorgasbord of details: often interesting, sometimes valuable, rarely irrelevant. Hence we begin with ethnic food consumption.

Ethnic food sales in Spain have long bubbled up from below, but only recently did salesmen rejoice over an upsurge in demand. Setting aside historical considerations, we point to the year 2000, when millions first heard the starting shot of mass immigration, and when Spain's ethnic food market first started to become a force to reckon. Ethnic food sales in Spain, recovering from a close brush with oblivion, totaled $220 million in 2005 and $470 million in 2009—all else being equal, this was projected to keep rising linearly until 2015.[12] Granted that "all else being equal" is a condition that hardly ever applies to economic reality, this well documented consumption increase of 3,100 percent in a decade proved anything but negligible, as swiftly evidenced by the rewriting of menus and the restocking of shelves in a scramble to satisfy such ballooning demand. More sales inspired a more diversified ethnic offering: pastries and dairy products followed shortly after the arrival of seasonings and snacks in supermarkets, while ethnic restaurants multiplied under the umbrella of Spain's street food restrictions, only to be soon joined by specialty shops offering ready-made ethnic meals for home consumption.[13] Spearheading this trend were Chinese and Mexican food, which jointly cap-

---

12. Dena M. Camarena and Ana I. Sanjuán, "El mercado de comida étnica en España," *Estudios Sociales* 16 (2008): 11.

13. Camarena and Sanjuán, "El mercado de comida étnica en España," 20.

tured 92 percent of ethnic food sales between 1999 and 2004, after which some Asian rivals, especially Indian food, began to gain ground. Ostensibly, in the account emerging from this number trail, ethnic food consumption in Spain followed sequentially from migration to popularity, and then continued consequentially from popularity to variety.[14]

An entirely invoice-based account of this progression can signal either confidence or complacency. But rather than recycling clichés about correlation and causation; and rather than conceiving of migration, popularity, and variety as inseparable; we can simply enrich this account by turning our attention from ethnic food consumption to ethnic food consumers. Surely, if only the newly arrived were consuming ethnic food, could this have hardly affected Spanish cuisine? The question is moot because the presupposition is false. Like the newly arrived, Spaniards had no permanent tastes, only a permanent appetite: from shifts in marketing campaigns to the exotic offers of catering services, ethnic food quickly expanded its native appeal to foreigners into a foreign appeal to natives. Variety proved instrumental, as socio-economically diverse natives were tempted with multiple possibilities for consumption, varying in ethnicity, price, venue, authenticity, and experience.[15] Behind this development were specialty shops, next to which there soon appeared Spanish-run shops plying the same trade, plus traditional restaurants dabbling in the business, all keen to compete for a slice of a market with such ethnically indiscriminate growth. Accordingly, to factor in this development, we turn our statistical gaze toward samples of the native agency involved in ethnic food consumption.

Statistical sampling is like tasting a pot of broth: if it has been well stirred, then a spoonful can convey the taste of the whole pot. Our spoonful here is the Spanish city of Zaragoza, where numerous surveys exploit the statistical fact that the average Zara-

---

14. Camarena and Sanjuán, "El mercado de comida étnica en España," 21.
15. Camarena and Sanjuán, "El mercado de comida étnica en España," 20.

gozan consumer behaves similarly to the average native Spanish consumer.[16] One of these surveys, the latest to burrow into the niche interest of ethnic food consumption, found in 2007 that 88.8 percent of respondents would describe themselves as "ethnic food consumers," with the reasons for their preferences ranging from flavor to price, novelty, and hassle-free preparation.[17] But the more solid this preference, the more fragmented it seemed to be. Twenty-five percent and 23 percent of native consumers favored Chinese and Mexican food, respectively, while 9 percent and 7.6 percent chose Indian and Japanese dishes, respectively, and dozens of piddling percentages cited miscellanea like Turkish, Greek, and Venezuelan cuisine.[18] Other surveys, those more commercially motivated, even elicited which ethnic foods respondents preferred, and here again the trend collapsed in on itself: restaurant dishes, take-home meals (including street food), and simple ingredients shared a more or less horizontal distribution. It stands to reason, therefore, that ethnic food variety was decisive in the zero-sum game of food consumption, with ethnic cuisine in Spain entailing a noticeable displacement of some big portions, for now unidentified, of Spanish cuisine.

Adapting Migratory Tastes via National Eating Habits

To this we must add the observation that so far we have only addressed the susceptibility of Spanish cuisine. Even if we could identify which foods were displaced, or what kind of Spaniard was more amenable to this dietary displacement, this would simply place more detail on a rather unbalanced account of Spain's culinary response to mass immigration. Hence our counterbalancing question. How resistant, or even assertive, was Spanish cuisine in

16. Eva Martínez-Salinas and Yolanda Polo-Redondo, "Comportamiento de compra familiar: Un contraste empírico para bienes de consumo duradero," *Cuadernos de Ciencias Económicas y Empresariales* 33 (1997): 90.
17. Camarena and Sanjuán, "El mercado de comida étnica en España," 24.
18. Camarena and Sanjuán, "El mercado de comida étnica en España," 25.

the face of mass immigration? To answer this, we have propped open the doors to immigrant homes and pried into whether, in any statistically significant sense, their culinary practices resembled Spanish eating habits. Granted that some resemblances were the product of habits directly imposed on the newly arrived, such as their training as domestic workers or restaurant staff, or their adherence to the late lunch and dinner times in Spain,[19] we concentrate on less forcefully enforced behavior by using two large-n studies, both resulting from a bizarre cooperation between Spain's Ministry of Agriculture and the Nielsen Corporation, to expose the meaningful consequences of Spanish cuisine on non-native eating habits.

The adapted diet of immigrants, for one, is pregnant with consequence. Surprisingly, some 50 percent of the newly arrived claimed in 2007 to have replaced basic foodstuffs from their diet since their arrival, with Central and South Americans most adaptive at 55 percent, and with Eastern Europeans and North Africans less so at 30 percent, perhaps because of an overlapping Mediterranean diet in the latter case.[20] Of note here are the replaced foodstuffs: couscous, mazamorra, local meat cuts, tropical fruits, and certain legumes and cereals, including a myriad of others subsumed under the label of "others," a label as opaque as it is suggestive of the surprising range of ethnic food variety that immigrants could not find in their adoptive country.[21] Life was hardly a bowl of cherries for this unlucky 50 percent, who had to make dietary adjustments because, reportedly, their desired ethnic products were unavailable (48 percent), or available but with an unfamiliar taste (31 percent),

---

19. Part of the reason might be time-related. Since Spanish clocks are perched on the western edge of the European Central Time (ECT) zone, Spaniards experience the natural sunrise-noon-sunset cycle at times that are considerably later than the corresponding times in most other ECT countries.
20. Spanish Ministry of Agriculture and Nielsen, *Hábitos alimentarios de los inmigrantes en España*, 131.
21. Spanish Ministry of Agriculture and Nielsen, *Hábitos alimentarios de los inmigrantes en España*, 131.

or available but simply too expensive (21 percent).[22] What makes this surprising is what compels us to touch on a thorny consistency issue: where was the sales-driven variety of ethnic food, which was marketed as such, being enjoyed by native consumers? If we assume that 50 percent was too high of a percentage to be unable to track down this variety, and if we give due consideration to the taste-related reason above, then it is possible that such ethnic food variety could have been targeted by and large at native consumers, inasmuch as non-native consumers, interestingly enough, proved to be receptive to Spanish cuisine.

Exactly how receptive depends on how far we can stretch our suspension of disbelief. In almost statistical unanimity, immigrants in Spain, whatever their ethnicity of origin in the regions of Central and South America, Eastern Europe, or North Africa, cited the paella as their favorite Spanish dish, a Valencian concoction widely regarded as Spain's national dish and deemed by most Spaniards as a local Valencian dish.[23] Similarly, 71 percent of immigrants in 2006, up from 64 percent in 2004, claimed to "quite like" or "really like" Spanish cuisine,[24] which understates even the average score of 3.9, along a 0-to-5 scale, that immigrants awarded to Spanish cuisine in other surveys.[25]

But it is here where our skepticism takes over: we consider that these expressions do not convey data so much as reassurance. Taste, much like happiness, lies behind an unquantifiable wall, one that we can only paint over with polysemic definitions, nebulous interpretations, arbitrary methodologies, dubious cor-

---

22. Spanish Ministry of Agriculture and Nielsen, *Hábitos alimentarios de los inmigrantes en España*, 134.

23. Lauroba and Ramos-Valverde, "Hábitos alimentarios de los inmigrantes en España," 45.

24. Spanish Ministry of Agriculture and Nielsen, *Hábitos alimentarios de los inmigrantes en España*, 141.

25. Lauroba and Ramos-Valverde, "Hábitos alimentarios de los inmigrantes en España," 45.

relations, and instinctive validation—problems that can detract from any self-respecting study, but that here amount to a pantomime of statistical reasoning. We therefore acknowledge that eating preferences, unlike other eating habits, are indeed impermeable to statistical analysis, a point in the broader lesson that descriptive statistics is valuable, not only because of the summary that it provides of what the world is like, but also because of the reminder that it offers of how important meta-statistical awareness can be. Until more trustworthy data becomes available, with the trustworthiness of this data based on its merits as well as on its sources, our observations are restricted to ethnic food variety and how, in its selectiveness, such variety exerted both intended and unintended effects. Precisely because ethnic food variety was intended mainly for native consumers and succeeded in appealing to various native palates, it unintendedly reduced the possibilities for ethnic food consumption by the newly arrived, thus facilitating a contraction of Spanish cuisine among natives and its startling expansion toward non-native eating habits.

A Culinary Exchange with an Economic Explanation

There is something unsettling about thinking of migratory flows as mere conveyor belts of ethnic cuisine. In an era of data-driven social science, we have become inured to thinking of the world as an aggregate of abstract flows, forces, and processes—abstractions that, lest we forget, are only statistical sketches of the lives of a bewildering assortment of individuals. Just as narcissism can misrepresent and dehumanize, so too can statistics. Even under the most favorable of circumstances, statistical analysis can enable us to build only a circumstantial case based on imperfect data. Hence our desire to tread very lightly among dehumanizing abstractions, especially those used as a validating veneer for an opinion, as we searched for clues as to the nature of collective misrepresentation.

But our findings are surprisingly inconsistent. By interpreting group behavior on the basis of abnormal individual behavior, we expected the falsehood of cuisine as an ethnic marker to prove uniformly responsive: either consistently pliable or consistently unyielding. Behind this expectation was the reasoning that a narcissist's exaggerations matter to him because little else does: that is, if revealed false, they would be swiftly abandoned; but until then, those exaggerations would remain as cornerstones of the Spanish large-group identity. Hardly could we have predicted that, through the action of the invisible hand of the market, the native ethno-national group would embrace cuisines partly abandoned by other ethno-national groups, cuisines that misrepresented them by being artificially targeted at natives. And neither could we have predicted that those other ethno-national groups would then embrace a cuisine partly abandoned by the native ethno-national group, a cuisine that misrepresented it by being artificially designed to exhibit only the most distinctive Spanish dishes to the world.

All of this appears to have become an exchange that normalized, or even trivialized, issues of ethnic representation and that ended up maximizing economic utility—the satisfaction of consumer needs and wants. If we then revisit our question, "how does the cuisine of an ethno-<u>national</u> group respond to the culinary practices introduced by mass immigration?" We are uncomfortably pressed to answer: "however the market determines such response to be." Where there is utility to be served, where cultural goods can be packaged and monetized, there it would seem that the artificiality of this ethnic marker is so utterly pervasive that, for most intents and purposes, ethnic representation becomes only an afterthought. Our discomfort with this conclusion arises from some of the simplifying assumptions of utility in economics, particularly the modeling of individuals as perfectly rational utility maximizers. This assumption disregards their proclivities to be forgetful, impulsive, resentful, passionate, self-centered, or shortsighted—flaws of our reasoning that are the core concern of psychology and that, in turn, are not yet fully assimilated into the very discipline that points us most clearly toward the answer.

We then seem to have entered an area of inquiry whose exploration requires both psychology and economics. If so, what implications could this have? Shall we then conceive the actors populating our analysis as hybrids between flawed individuals and interacting robots? Is creative destruction not only the preservation of market economies, but also the driving force behind the reformulation of culinary preferences? Or are we extrapolating too much from two variables in one case study? Should we select an ethno-national group less open to facile criticism? Or should we discard our constructivist understanding of "ethnic marker"? And might there be other personality disorders that, regardless of utility, could prompt an ethno-national group to retain or relinquish its culinary practices? Needless to say, these are merely our questions. Our hope is that by now the readers will have more of their own.

Bibliography

Arango, Joaquín. *Exceptional in Europe? Spain's Experience with Immigration and Integration.* Washington, DC: Migration Policy Institute, 2013.

Bartlett, Steven J. "Narcissism and Philosophy." *Methodology and Science* 19 (1986): 16–26.

Brown, Andrew D. "Narcissism, Identity and Legitimacy." *Academy of Management Review* 22 (1997): 643–86.

Camarena, Dena M. "El mercado de comida étnica en España." *Estudios Sociales* 16 (2008): 8–37.

González-Enriquez, Carmen. "Spain." In *European Immigration: A Sourcebook*, edited by Anna Triandafyllidou and Ruby Gropas, 321–34. Aldershot: Ashgate Publishing Limited, 2007.

Lauroba, Ignacio. "Hábitos alimentarios de los inmigrantes en España." *Investigación y Marketing* 89 (2005): 42–48.

Martínez-Salinas, Eva. "Comportamiento de compra familiar: Un contraste empírico para bienes de consumo duradero." *Cuadernos de Ciencias Económicas y Empresariales* 33 (1997): 85–110.

Esther M. Rebato-Ochoa. "Las nuevas culturas alimentarias: Globalización vs. etnicidad." *Osasunaz* 10 (2009): 135–39.

Spanish Ministry of Agriculture, Fishing and Food and Nielsen Corporation. *Hábitos alimentarios de los inmigrantes en España.* Madrid: Fotocomposición SA, 2007.

van den Berghe, Pierre L. "Ethnic Cuisine: Culture in Nature." *Ethnic and Racial Studies* 7 (1984): 387–97.

Volkan, Vamik D. "Transgenerational Transmissions and Chosen Traumas: An Aspect of Large-Group Identity." *Group Analysis* 34 (2001): 79–97.

Wimmer, Andreas. "The Making and Unmaking of Ethnic Boundaries." *American Journal of Sociology* 113 (2008): 970–1022.

Fetish, Nation-building and Hummus: The Fetishization of Street Food throughout Israel's Nation-building Process

Martina Salakova

Baruch Spinoza suggested that as humans become less and less attached to nature, the necessity of a fetish becomes bigger and the suspicion of a higher principle rises. This essay attempts to disentangle the web of Israel's world of street food and the significance it plays in building and maintaining an imagined national identity in terms of a fetish. The food that we eat publicly—most ubiquitously street food—is a metaphor for what is de-facto socially accepted or not. The evolution of what is socially accepted can be seen as a role-playing game with a variety of actors, a game in which the objects of consumption only get their form in the process of role-playing—their semiotic value externally ascribed by their use. What do we then observe in how others play, what others eat? Is this the same case with a fetish, one that we acquire by watching others? To better understand the rules of this imagined game in Israel, we will have a closer look at food consumption since the very early Zionist movements; its socialist character that neglected private eating; and also street food. The main question raised is: How did Israel's street food landscape come to be dominated by a limited number of Arab dishes?

What constitutes a fetish? The history of this term is that of othering processes, the *other* being mystified, condemned for sorcery, primitivism and such. But a fetish, according to Hegel, helps protect the self from the feared outside world, nature, and the feared unknown that we yearn to control. A fetish helps us feel safe. Freud adds that the pervert—and essentially to a certain point we are all perverts—needs this separating medium in order to be able to exist within a conundrum of both disavowing and affirming a threatening reality. The prototypical fetish arises, according to Freud, from a son's perceived castration of his mother and shields his ego from the threat of his own potential castration by absorbing the interest he had ascribed to the phallus.[1] The primary emphasis here is the substitution that occurs in the process of fetishization. This object can be the shoes that we wear every day, the table that we build as carpenters, or the food that we consume.

This essay will follow the assumption that a dish as a fetish comforts a state during its nation-building process, as it attempts to distinguish itself from other nations. It does so in a very unique way, as the country is, except for the Palestinian population, almost entirely based on immigration. Israel, being a reasonably young state, whose existence is an issue of permanent international controversy, is under constant pressure to prove itself—also in terms of food. Cultural battles are fought internally and externally, the so-called Hummus Wars, a symbolic fight over who invented this delicious dip, being an example. The self-declared Jewish state was always more than "just" Jewish—apart from numerous religious minorities, it holds today 1.7 million Muslim Arabs, which constitute more than 20 percent of the population, with percentages rising each year due to a higher birth rate. In addition, *Jewish* is an overly simplified marker that scarcely lives up to the pluralism of the migrant backgrounds of Jewish Israelis.

To continue unravelling of parts in the net of Israeli's world of street food, this essay searches for the reasons why Israeli street food has been Arab-inspired from its infancy. A country whose official culture is predominantly Ashkenazi, and as such a young country that would seem to be in strong need of a nationalized identity, why would undeniably Arab dishes fill the most public area of food consumption—street food?

---

1. Sigmund Freud, "Fetishism," trans. J. Strachey, in *The Standard Edition of the Complete Psychological Works of Sigmund Freud* (London: Hogarth and the Institute of Psychoanalysis, 1953–74), 21:153–55.

Another side of the coin can be shown by eating habits of the *Haredim,* the ultra-orthodox who, due to a passage in the Torah, condemn eating in public and see street food as dirty and unhygienic. Plenty of Israeli Haredim would refer to themselves as non-Zionist, or even anti-Zionist, but their involvement in Israeli culture and politics is not to be underestimated.

It seems that Israel has experienced more uncertainty about its secular and national identity in the last decades. When, in 1948, the borders of Israel were defined, Ben-Gurion and his associates did not seem to mind that the Temple Mount, the most sacred place in the world in Judaism, fell on the Jordanian side of the border. In fact, they were much keener to preserve Mount Scopus, which was to hold the future Hebrew University of Jerusalem. In the last decades, colonizing processes have become much more religion-orientated, such as the inclusion of religious sites on the Israeli side of the West Bank Wall, for instance, the Tomb of Rachel, one of the four symbolical matriarchs of the Hebrew nation, about whom one can read in the book of Genesis. If this place was so important back then, why was it not included in the new borders of 1967 and only included when building the separation barrier in the 2000s? It is, after all, very close to Jewish areas like Gilo, a neighborhood in East-Jerusalem, which was indeed annexed. Another example is the Tomb of Samuel, the Last Judge, one of the prophets of the ancient Hebrews, northwest of another such a neighborhood, Ramot: The Tomb of Samuel was also just left out of the annexation border. One could guess that the Israeli leadership back in 1967, a self-perceived liberal and secular leadership, thought that those places were not worth the trouble, as they are also holy for Muslims. In fact, at the time, it might have looked like Israeli society would become less and less religious, less and less orthodox, over time. However, the opposite has been the case.

But let us set the politics aside and talk food. For the purpose of this essay I use the term *fetish* to rethink symbols of national identity as artifacts—as edible artifacts. A theoretician from the field of psychoanalysis might be of aid to make this connection: Wilfred Ruprecht Bion offers the theory that we offload different emotions into persons or objects. The chosen persons or objects are hence subjected to simultaneous control and adoration.[2] Another theoretician, Vamık D. Volkan, who is also discussed in Ivan Ovejero's article with reference to ethno-narcissism, associates with Volkan and further emphasizes how, what he calls "shared objects", such as food, help to create a group identity. In addition, the sociologist Pierre Bourdieu acknowledged that flavor is also not just a matter of taste, but rather an element in a "struggle over classifications", a strategic mechanism, that organizes social divisions.[3]

A fetish is an object, alive or non-alive, to which we attach certain attributes, which it would not have in its natural state. For instance a piece of carved wood to which someone attaches the attribute that it can cause a rain shower.[4] In addition, it can bring specific details into the foreground and cast others into the background.[5] The diachronic development of the semantic meaning of the term 'fetish' reflects how Western observers have included the other, even to such an extent, that they started to ask themselves about their own "otherness."[6] The term was first used by Portuguese merchants and sailors who, on encountering West African religious rites, reported on the worship of religious and cultural objects. The practices of this specific "other" were considered weird

---

2. W. R. Bion, *Experiences in Groups and other Papers* (London: Tavistock, 1961).

3. Pierre Bourdieu, *Distinction: A Social Critique of the Judgement of Taste* (Cambridge: Harvard University Press, 1984).

4. Stephan Grigat, "Kritik des Fetischismus: Die Marxsche Werttheorie als Grundlage emanzipativer Gesellschaftskritik" (Diploma Thesis, University of Vienna, 1997), 20.

5. Louise J. Kaplan, *Cultures of Fetishism* (New York: Palgrave Macmillan, 2006), 6.

6. Alfonso Iacono, "Fetischismus und Substitution," in *Fetisch als heuristische Kategorie: Geschichte – Rezeption – Interpretation*, ed. Christine Antenhofer (Bielefeld: Transcript Verlag, 2011), 85.

and uncivilized, and the meaning of the objects was considered to be a substitution for a higher principle that they believed in, the Christian God. A remarkable turn in the term's meaning occurred with Marx and his followers, who shifted the focus of being on the "other" to the "own." The "commodity fetishism," which Marx coined, again differs from the Freudian perspective to the term. The main difference between the Marxian and the Freudian fetish is the question, whether a fetish is perceived consciously. In contrast to Freud's sexual fetish theories, Marx postulates that a commodity fetish is characterized by people not perceiving it consciously, thus enabling a critical approach to societies' structures. The value of the commodity fetish is more worth than the object itself. It exists only because it's an expression of societal relations or, as one can put it, the "reification of social relations."[7]

I argue that nation-building processes come with fetishist reflections of the constructed self and that food and, considered here specifically, street food is a part of this. As is the case in other nations, Israel has gone under the process of inventing itself and still is, and this task requires the permanent demarcation of an "other" and a playful assembling of what is to be a part of this nation's image and what is not.

The most thorough, albeit short analysis on the history of Israeli street food was published fifteen years ago, and few studies have been done on Israeli street food consumption patterns.[8] The authors of that analysis argue that Israeli street food landscape is characterized by three aspects: the absence of street vendors in

---

7. Stephan Grigat, "Der Marx'sche Fetischbegriff und seine Bedeutung für eine Kritik des Antisemitismus," in *Fetisch als heuristische Kategorie: Geschichte – Rezeption – Interpretation*, ed. Christina Antenhofer (Bielefeld: Transcript Verlag, 2011), 277; and Grigat, "Kritik des Fetischismus," 22.

8. Liora Gvion-Rosenberg and Naomi Troslter, "Street Food Vending: The Israeli Scenario," in *Street Foods, World Review of Nutrition and Dietetics* 86, ed. Artemis P. Simopoulos and Ramesh Venkataramana Bhat (Washington, DC: Karger, 2000).

major cities in favor of institutionalized and small businesses, a lack of an ethnic-orientated food economy, and the low number of women working as street vendors. The culinary street food scene is dominated by Falafel, sunflower seeds, nuts, ice cream, and pizza. Since the 1980s they observe a "growing social legitimacy for immigrants to express and develop their individual ethnic identity", allowing for the "gradual introduction and acceptance of ethnic foods" that added sambusak, couscous, Druze Pita, "Arab delights" like Baklava, and different Russian breads to the range of Israeli cities' street foods.[9] This trend was preceded by a decade's-long atmosphere of neglect towards a broad range of street foods mainly owed to the Zionist agenda.

Food culture played an important role for the European Zionists who migrated to Palestine before the foundation of Israel in 1948 and continued to play this role during the constitution of a national identity, its collective memory, and political aspirations.[10] The early Zionists brought with them a cuisine that already showed entanglements with the cuisines of the areas they came from, usually in line with Jewish dietary customs and rules. So, even if a collective Jewish food existed, their mixed countries of origin and the different degrees of their integration in their home countries made for a varied food line-up. Little of this food survived the program of the early Zionists. In their new ideology, there was little understanding for keeping the culture of the *Galut* (diaspora/exile)—an atmosphere in which, mildly put, a lot of anti-Semitism was experienced, in the quest for a Jewish national project.

The new food was a product of several influences, mainly local Arab foods. Early on, the Zionist project was building separate communities with a clear distinction from the local Arabs, however this process changed from demarcation to appropria-

---

9. Gvion-Rosenberg and Troslter, "Street Food Vending," 161.
10. Ronald Ranta and Yonatan Mendel, "Consuming Palestine: Palestine and Palestinians in Israeli Food Culture," in *Ethnicities* 14, no. 3 (2014).

tion—according to Ronald Ranta and Yonatan Mendel, whose writing comes from a strict anti-colonialist perspective, the Arab influence was recoded as belonging to the Zionist settlers.[11] This was eased by the perspective that Jews who have Arab origins were said to have brought food traditions with them.[12] Ranta and Mendel examined cook books from the 1930s to the 1950s and sadly found that Hummus, Falafel, and Tahini were either presented as Israeli, Mizrahi, or Sephardic food.[13] However, one must note that this strict colonialist perspective that concentrates on the appropriation of the culture of the oppressed to the culture of the oppressor can be a very limiting perspective, especially to foreign writers, and tends to oversimplify history for a political agenda.

The ongoing imbalance of power puts Palestinian Arabs at a disadvantage in Israeli public participation. This inequality also puts researchers in a difficult position. Liora Gvion, a food sociologist based in Tel Aviv, writes of her difficulties in conducting research within the Palestinian community. Gvion is one of three writers who have promoted dealing with the subject of food culture to include Palestinians, these writers all are Jewish-Israelis. Palestinian reactions to her newest book *Beyond Hummus and Falafel* were very critical, due to the fact that a "Jewish woman 'dared writing about our food'", or that they "were tired of being folklorized and looked down on." One of her interviewees states that she "thought that you [Gvion] were just another female journalist coming to ask, take notes, and write about our food in the paper as if we were Eskimos."[14]

---

11. Nathan Marom, "Relating A City's History and Geography with Bourdieu: One Hundred Years of Spatial Distinction in Tel Aviv," *International Journal of Urban and Regional Research* 38, no. 4 (2014).

12. Ronald Ranta and Yonatan Mendel, "Consuming Palestine," in *Ethnicities* 14, no. 3 (2015), 420.

13. Ranta and Mendel, "Consuming Palestine," 419.

14. Liora Gvion, *Beyond Hummus and Falafel: Social and Political Aspects of Palestinian Food in Israel* (Berkeley: University of California Press, 2000), 2.

Many sources state that Palestinian cuisine was romanticized and folklorized by early Zionists and that this view has structurally entered the collective imaging of the Palestinian other. In fact, a study of tourism in Palestinian areas of Israel shows that state agencies foster a commodification of Palestinian traditional culture. It is a tendency that Palestinian culture is portrayed as being a culture that did not quite catch the train of modernity—that lags and is poor. This is false. In several thorough studies, Gvion has shown that modernity did not skip the Palestinians when it comes to food. As tradition dialogues with modernity, Palestinian kitchens have modernized equipment and have not ignored the influence that the access to diversified commodities has brought about. Modernity is not seen as a threat to perceived traditional Palestinian culture by the Palestinian community in Israel.

The next question is why the so dominantly Arab Israeli street food is limited to just a small range of dishes. Certainly the Palestinian cuisine has more to offer than Hummus, Taboule, Falafel, and grilled meats. Menus of Palestinian street vendors and restaurants all look very much alike, no matter where one goes. Two patterns are observable as means of explanation: one is that the dishes are prepared by Palestinian men rather than women. Men dominate the public food sphere, hence strongly limiting women's participation in the public realm, whereas a woman's cooking labor happens predominantly at home. As such, a strong distinction happens between home and outside food. It is considered disrespectful toward the woman's kitchen labor to eat out. This mindset can be exemplified through plenty of interviews. One cook, who was interviewed by Gvion, is among them:

> If I listed meluhiye or olesh on the menu, my clients would laugh at me. They eat it at home all the time. Why would they order it in a restaurant? At a restaurant people order shawarma, shishlik, kebobs, and never a dish that our women prepare. My clients respect their

wives and want to treat them by taking them out. I respect our women and therefore I never serve dishes that women prepare at home. I want them to feel like queens on their day off.[15]

The second aspect of why only a handful of Arab dishes are served by Palestinians that should be emphasized is intertwined with the first. It is again a matter of identity and fetishization. The fact that dishes that are traditionally served at home are not shared with the public is a form of protecting their own distinct social relations.

Eating street food has never enjoyed high popularity in Israel, even in times of economic hardship in the 1950s and 1960s, when there might have been a higher demand for culturally appropriate, low-cost food.[16] Apart from climatic and economic factors (such as subsidized meals) I dare to speak of a confusion, of what is to be socially accepted to eat in public, as the national foods Hummus and Falafel are so disputed and the dietary customs, especially during times of religious festivities, are very strict.

To conclude, it can be stated that Israel's street food history demonstrates the protective character of a fetish as well as its function to order social relations between the self and the other. When walking its baby steps the future-to-be state of Israel installed a cultural program of neglecting culinary practices of the arriving migrants in favor of local Arab foods. These foods were either romanticized or their appropriation eased by Arab backgrounds of Jewish arrivals in a quest for creating an authority over a dish's authenticity. This authority helped the arrivals feel safe in their new cultural setting. When in the 1980s the approval of immigrants' ethnic backgrounds grew stronger, it seems that the culinary identity of Israel has grown more confident thus allow-

---

15. Liora Gvion, "Intertwining Tradition with Modernity: The Case of Palestinian Restaurants in Israel," *Journal of Intercultural Studies* 35, no. 4 (2014), 372.
16. Gvion-Rosenberg and Troslter, "Street Food Vending," 167.

ing for new dishes to enter the street food sphere without feeling threatened. Inner-Jewish debates on adhering to dietary customs complicate the matter.

I argue that there are very homogenous food fetishization processes, the secular every-day Israeli having a different approach than an orthodox Haredi, who might also see their own, strict view on dietary customs as a shield against the secular. The gravity of the emotions that are offloaded into these edible fetish artifacts become clear when looking at the heated debates on the origins of dishes like Hummus, on how Palestinians react to studies on their food, or how Palestinians attempt to protect their own food culture from intrusions. Hopefully this article can be seen as a stimulating contribution to debates on Israeli street food and the heuristic value of the concept of fetishes.

Bibliography

Ansky, Sherry, and Nelli Sheffer. *The Food of Israel: Authentic Recipes from the Land of Milk and Honey.* Singapore: Periplus Editions, 2000.

Avieli, Nir, and Rafi Grosglik. "Food and Power in the Middle East and the Mediterranean." *Food, Culture and Society* 16, no. 2 (2013): 181–195.

Bion, Wilfried Ruprecht. *Experiences in Groups and other Papers.* London: Tavistock, 1961. Accessed February 10, 2015. http://www. pep-web.org/document.php?id=zbk.006.0001a.

Bourdieu, Pierre. *Distinction: A Social Critique of the Judgement of Taste.* Cambridge: Harvard University Press, 1984.

Endevelt, Ronit. "School Lunch Programs in Israel, Past and Present." *Hygiea Internationalis* 6, no. 1 (2007): 93–105.

Freud, Sigmund. "Fetishism." Translated by J. Strachey. Vol. 21 of *The Standard Edition of the Complete Psychological Works of Sigmund Freud.* London: Hogarth and the Institute of Psychoanalysis, 1953–74.

Grigat, Stephan. Kritik des Fetischismus: Die Marxische Werttheorie als Grundlage emanzipativer Gesellschaftskritik. Diploma thesis, University of Vienna, 1997.

———. "Der Marx'sche Fetischbegriff und seine Bedeutung für eine Kritik des Antisemitismus." In *Fetisch als heuristische Kategorie: Geschichte – Rezeption – Interpretation*, edited by Christina Antenhofer, 275–92. Bielefeld: Transcript Verlag, 2011.

Gvion, Liora. *Beyond Hummus and Falafel: Social and Political Aspects of Palestinian Food in Israel.* Berkeley: University of California Press, 2012.

———. "Cooking, Food, and Masculinity. Palestinian Men in Israeli Society." *Men and Masculinities* 14, no. 4 (2011): 408–29.

———. "Cuisines of Poverty as Means of Empowerment: Arab Food in Israel." *Agriculture and Human Values* 23, no. 3 (2006): 299–312.

———. "Intertwining Tradition with Modernity: The Case of Palestinian Restaurants in Israel." *Journal of Intercultural Studies* 35, no. 4 (2014): 366–84. doi:10.1080/07256868.2014.913010.

———. "Narrating Modernity and Tradition: The Case of Palestinian Food in Israel." *Identities: Global Studies in Culture and Power* 16, no. 4 (2009): 391–413. doi:10.1080/10702890903020869.

Gvion-Rosenberg, Liora, and Naomi Trostler. "Street Food Vending: The Israeli Scenario." In *Street Foods. World Review of Nutrition and Dietetics* 86, edited by Artemis P. Simopoulous and Ramesh Venkataramana Bhat, 155–168. Washington, D.C.: Karger, 2000.

Helman, Anat. "European Jews in the Levant Heat: Climate and Culture in 1920s and 1930s Tel Aviv." *Journal of Israeli History: Politics, Society, Culture* 22, no. 1 (March 2003): 71–90.

Iacono, Alfonso, M. "Fetischismus und Substitution." In *Fetisch als heuristische Kategorie: Geschichte – Rezeption – Interpretation*, edited by Christina Antenhofer. Bielefeld: Transcript Verlag, 2011.

Kaplan, Louise J. *Cultures of Fetishism.* New York: Palgrave Macmillan, 2006.

Kraig, Bruce, and Taylon Colleen Sen, eds. *Street Food around the World: An Encyclopedia of Food and Culture.* Santa Barbara: ABC-Clio, 2013.

Marom, Nathan. "Relating A City's History and Geography with Bourdieu: One Hundred Years of Spatial Distinction in Tel Aviv." *International Journal of Urban & Regional Research* 38, no. 4 (2014): 1344–62.

Ranta, Ronald, and Yonatan Mendel. "Consuming Palestine: Palestine and Palestinians in Israeli Food Culture." *Ethnicities* 14, no. 3 (2014): 412–35.

Americanized Taco:
A Mere Adjustment of the Mexican Cuisine to Los Angeles's Palate?

Julia Rott

In discussing Mexican street food its great variety is worth noting, including chalupas, elotes, gorditas, tamales, empalmes, tostadas, tlayudas, tacos, soups, and tortas. Chalupas, tlayudas, and toastadas are a type of tortilla; elote means corn on the cob; gorditas are small savory cakes; tamales are a traditional Mesoamerican dish consisting of dough stuffed with a hot dish and steamed or boiled in a leaf wrapper; and empalmes as well as tortas are a form of sandwich. The above only offer the briefest of glimpses into the rich Mexican cuisine. As such, it is beyond the scope of this paper to adequately address all of these foods in such a limited space, therefore I focus on tacos including burritos and tortillas as one example of how dishes become transformed to gain recognition beyond national boundaries by the process of migration.

I decided to focus on Los Angeles, because it offered me a wide range of sources, and, finally, decided to limit my paper to Mexican migration and the Mexican American community in the area. Los Angeles is, for many reasons, hallmarked by cultural and ethnic diversity, and my intention is to explore how this affects the local street food trends. My goal in this essay is to analyze the relationship between Mexican and American cuisine and to expose how migration has influenced the street food through the present. I aim to determine whether there was an adjustment of the imported culinary particularities of Mexican Americans to the local food habits. My main argument is that the tacos many Americans know are not Mexican food among the majority of Mexicans. To gain a closer look at current developments, it is necessary to include a historical view of the migration of people, foods, as well as the changing culinary identity dating back to pre-colonial times. With this in mind, the discussion consists of three chapters as follows: Glen Bell, the Mexican community and global phenomenon; Mexica heritage, Mexican cookery and Californian cuisine; and struggle, cultural differentiation and the culinary amalgamation.[1] Despite this wide timeframe, my prime focus lies on the twentieth century up to now.

In his book *Planet Taco: A Global History of Mexican Food*, Jeffrey M. Pilcher states that one of the top three ethnic foods in the United States is Mexican.[2] However, when Mexicans and Americans talk about Mexican food, they often are not speaking about the same type of cuisine. Pilcher examines the question of what original Mexican food really encompasses. He concludes that the concept of "authentic" Mexican cuisine has been contrived by promoters of culinary tourism and encompasses a heterogeny of culinary traditions. The result was the formation of a new type of cuisine, California Mexican cooking, as an adaptation to the American palate. A lecture by Andrew Smith presented at Oregon State University in 1999 titled *Tacos, Enchiladas and Refried Beans: the Invention of Mexican American Cookery* provides a historical view of the Mexican food culture illuminating its Aztec heritage and following through the cuisine's current Americanization.[3] Arjun Appadurai's idea of the tension between cultural homogenization

1. The term "mexica" reflects the self-denomination of the Nahua-speaking people in ancient Mexico, whereas the term "Aztec" comes from the myth of Azlán and was not used among the mexicas themselves, but served as a denomination among colonialists and scholars of Mesoamerican culture. J. Richard Andrews, *Introduction to Classical Nahuatl*, rev. ed. (Norman, OK: University of Oklahoma Press, 2003).

2. Jeffery M. *Pilcher, Planet Taco: A Global History of the Mexican Food* (New York: Oxford University Press, 2012).

3. Andrew Smith, "Tacos, Enchiladas and Refried Beans: The Invention of Mexican-American Cookery," (presentation, Cultural and Historical Aspects of Foods - Yesterday, Today, and Tomorrow, Oregon State University, April 9–11, 1999), http://web.archive.org/web/20070404220418/http://food.oregonstate.edu/ref/culture/mexico_smith.html.

and heterogenization is helpful in approaching such a contradiction of authenticity and adoption. The first of his "five dimensions of global cultural flows," which he calls *ethnoscape*, illustrates how moving groups deeply shape the world which we live in.[4] Newspaper articles such as "Mexican Street Food in Los Angeles" and "L.A. Food Culture Offers a Glimpse into 'The New America'" made it possible to include current street food trends within Los Angeles in addition to the historical roots of Mexican food.

Glen Bell, the Mexican Community, and the Global Phenomenon

In the United States, the word "taco" is strongly connected with Glen Bell (1923–2010) who claimed himself to be the father of the fast-food-taco. He actually transformed Mexican food from belonging to an ethnic community into a highly commercialized product gaining nation-wide prominence. Inspired by the McDonald brothers, Richard and Maurice, Bell sought a market niche in Mexican food. In 1951, he sold his first tacos for nineteen cents, after that he created a dish consisting of fried taco shells with his chili-dog sauce replacing the original handmade salsa. In 1962, finally, Bell opened the first shop of the now famous Taco Bell fast-food chain. Although it seems today that Glen Bell launched an impressive taco empire, from the perspective of the 1950s, Bell was a "little fish" in the food industry: dependent on the Mexican community for both the tortillas which he fried into shells and further advice for his menu. In fact, Mexican Americans invented the Americanized taco as an expression of divided local kitchens by adapting their foods to a changing society.[5]

---

4. Arjun Appadurai, *Modernity at Large: Cultural Dimension of Globalization* (Minneapolis: University of Minnesota Press, 1996), 33.
5. Gustavo Arellano, *Taco USA: How Mexican Food Conquered America* (New York: Scribner, 2013), 61–63.

In their essay *Ethnic Migration, Assimilation, and Consumption*, Melanie Wallendorf and Michael Reilly focus on the cross-cultural comparison considering the effect of the Mexican Americans' culture of origin and culture of residence. What Carlos Vélez-Ibáñez presents in his book *Border Visions* as a "bumping process" of one group into one another is also mentioned in this paper. He attempts to bring their histories together and to understand the process by which immigrants moved into the American Southwest and created a sense of cultural space, and how others defined, denied, or accepted this cultural space through the creation of boundaries.[6] Thus, these novel styles of cooking can be seen as a combination of Mexican culture and North American ingredients developed by immigrants and ethnic chefs mirroring an upcoming Mexican American identity.

As early as the first decades of the twentieth century, Mexican Americans started to call for civil rights, and during and after World War II they were empowered by employment opportunities including military service. With their increasing earnings, they changed their diets and became involved in culinary tourism. Those developments resulted in street vendors becoming a place to go for Mexican food, rather than formal restaurants in cities such as San Antonio or Los Angeles, which have been among the leading urban centers of Mexican American life.[7] It would not be until the 1980s, that Los Angeles would experience a revival of the Mexican community that exceeded the height of cultural impact they achieved in 1930. But even at its peak in the 1920s, and for decades afterward, the Mexican community in Los Angeles failed to reach the power to impede the white, Protestant dominance of the city's symbolic economy. With a few Spanish-language radio stations, newspapers, and other sort of media, the Mexican community was depending

6. Carlos G. Vélez-Ibáñez, *Border Visions: Mexican Cultures of the Southwest United States* (Tucson: The University of Arizona Press, 1996), 6.
7. Pilcher, *Planet Taco*, 130–31.

on popular cultural forms to create an idea of group identity and to establish symbols demarcating that identity. During the 1950s and 1960s, there was a revival of a Mexican cultural ego in East L.A. preceded by the numerous food stalls of the First Street Mercado. Crucial to this ego formation was the narrative of a geographic, culinary birthplace—Mexico City. The adoption of *pescaderías* serving steaming bowls of seafood and the Mexico-City-style *taquerías* offering *tacos al pastor*, a typical street food in Mexico City, resulting from a fusion of Lebanese style similar to the Turkish Döner kebab or Greek gyros, constituted new spaces for the social perception of Mexican identity.[8]

The images of pauperized chili queens as patrons for Mexican cuisine were replaced by community leaders, offering on the one hand a place to gather for insiders and on the other hand an upstanding public face to outsiders. The restaurants as well as the street vendors called their foods "Mexican" rather than Cal-Mex or Tex-Mex. Nevertheless, many Mexicans were not inclined to recognize these new forms of food as authentic; this did not, however, diminish the popularity of the dishes. Previously divided supply chains for ethnic enclaves and mainstream stores were joined toward an emerging Mexican American demand by means of cross-cultural exchange and experimentation.[9] Basically, the nature of these Mexican American regional cuisines was neither due to the sole merit of Mexican cooks nor outsiders like Glen Bell but in fact the competition between the two. Essential steps of this process of cultural formation were the postwar expansion of consumerism, restaurants and food processing. Ethnic foods developed rapidly, and while Mexican cooks adjusted their recipes for a mass audience, restaurants and food processors outside the Mexican community sought to make innovations like tacos attractive to consumers.

---

8. Victor M. Valle and Rodolfo D. Torres, *Latino Metropolis*, Globalization and Community 7 (Minneapolis: University of Minnesota, 2000), 84.
9. Pilcher, *Planet Taco*, 131.

The Americanized taco can be understood as a global phenomenon resulting from the interplay between insiders: those of Mexican origin; and the outsiders, the American adaptation. One way in which Mexican cookery became significant in American cuisine was through *braceros*, migrant Mexican farm workers, who brought their foodways with them when travelling to the United States. Mexican seasonal workers in the fields of California were carriers of this culinary invasion, later spreading through urban centers like San Francisco, San Diego and Los Angeles. In his book *Modernity at Large*, Appadurai states that the relationship between cultural homogenization and cultural heterogenization presents a major difficulty in current global interplays. Within his concept he creates "five dimensions of global flows," the first of which being the *ethnoscape*. By *ethnoscape*, Appadurai means the people who shape the changing world "which we live in: tourists, immigrants, refugees, exiles, seasonal workers, and other moving groups and individuals constitute an essential feature of the world and appear to affect the politics of (and between) nations to a hitherto unprecedented degree."[10] That does not imply that there are no steady communities and networks of kinfolk, friendship, birth, abode, and other filial forms; but rather, that all of these stabilities are marked by human movements as more groups and individuals are confronted with the fact of having to move in reality or of wanting to as an expectation. Within Appadurai's *ethnoscape*, the Mexican American community can be examined as the larger entity and the Mexican street vendors as the smaller one, which both apply to street food developments in Los Angeles.[11]

In the twentieth century, the United States grew as a global economic power and simultaneously brought Tex-Mex as well as the Cal-Mex cooking into the wider world. During the Cold War, when people acquainted with the Cal-Mex cuisine began to travel,

---

10. Appadurai, *Modernity at Large*, 33.
11. Appadurai, *Modernity at Large*, 33.

they took with them their knowledge about tacos and burritos, and the globalization of Mexican food was underway. American hegemony carried ethnic cuisine with it. This global migration was initiated by two particular groups who had the power to do so: firstly, surfers, who traveled to find waves and iconically drank Corona and ate tacos on Baja California beaches and secondly, the U.S. military personal stationed in the Southwest. Essentially, the concept of the taco shell was used to develop an international market for Mexican food. It began a transformation from the hard taco into a soft wheat flour tortilla, which became more common in the United States than its Mexican fellow. Ethnic stereotypes as well as its appearance, defined the postwar connotation with the taco shell.[12]

Mexican Heritage, Mexican Cookery, and Californian Cuisine

Pilcher discusses the limitations of defining authenticity in a culinary way and argues that concepts of "authentic" Mexican cuisine have been contrived by supporters of culinary tourism. In pre-Hispanic or colonial times, such a cuisine did not exist, although it is often ascribed to ancient Aztecs and Mayas. Indeed, it was the outcome of globalization, beginning with the Spanish conquest—like the Mexican nation itself.[13] Facing the threat of losing their culinary identity to their influential neighbor, Mexicans started to seek the roots of their national cuisine in the pre-Hispanic past, relying on the so called "Aztec heritage." The Mexicas based their cuisine on maize and the culinary heritage of the people they conquered. For them, as well as for the Mayas, maize was holy and its various forms played important roles in their diets. With the Spanish conquest in 1521, various cookery techniques and ingredients arrived at the New World by way of the colonists. An important cooking technique, which

12. Pilcher, *Planet Taco*, 11–13.
13. Pilcher, *Planet Taco*, 221–22.

had been unknown in the pre-Columbian times, was frying. For many Mexicans, frying became a very significant way of cooking that permanently changed their cuisine to include crisp tortillas, refried beans, and other fried, bread-like foods. In 1821, Mexico gained independence from Spain, and the culinary arts prospered. By then, Mexican cookery was surrounded by Mexican, Spanish, and international components, including dishes that became common in the United States, such as tamales, tortillas, and enchiladas. In 1845, the United States annexed Texas and secured California and the American Southwest in the aftermath of the Mexican-American War. Thus, the United States not only gained a vast new territory but also a multi-cultural empire consisting of thousands of Spanish-speaking people. The cuisine of these people was not homogenous at all and differed distinctly from the way the majority of Americans were used to cooking.[14]

Over time, more and more elements of the former Mexican cuisine became evident in Anglo-American way of eating. In order to address a larger amount of people in the United States, Mexican foods were adapted to the American palate. Besides the well-known Tex-Mex, many other regional Mexican American cooking styles arose. Originating in the San Francisco Bay Area in the 1970s, and later spreading through Los Angeles, the West Coast produced a culinary revolution called "Californian cuisine" emphasizing its European and Pacific Rim recipes and ingredients. Shortly afterwards, Los Angeles started to savor its Mexican and Native American influences.[15] While in Texas the cooks strived to preserve their relation to Mexico, in California the authenticity of an emerging, self-consciously distinct, regional cuisine rested on connections to Old California. The staple of Cal-Mex was the taco. It permeated into California, especially during the 1930s and 1940s. Like the English term sandwich, in Mexico, the word taco

---

14. Smith, "Tacos, Enchiladas and Refried Beans," 1–5.
15. Valle and Torres, *Latino Metropolis*, 86.

was a general term. Basically, Mexican taco meant any food rolled, folded or fried into tortillas that is consumed by hand. The filling consists of various ingredients like beef, egg, tomato, pork, chicken, lettuce, onions, beans, cheese, chili sauce, and guacamole. Whereas the Mexican taco usually is soft-shelled, the Americanized version is made by the hard, U-shaped crisp fried tortilla, sold by many restaurants, fast food chains as well as street vendors. Another very prominent icon of California's Mexican cooking is the burrito. Andrew Smith states in his lecture that the first time *burrito* was seen printed in America was in 1934 having its origin somewhere between Tucson and Los Angeles.[16] During the 1930s, it was sold throughout Los Angeles, becoming popular in Mexican American cuisine in other parts of California in the 1950s and gaining nation-wide recognition in the 1960s. Only with time, as a result of adaption, the burritos assumed their modern Americanized form wrapped in large, wheat flour tortillas.[17]

The curious development of the burrito can be explained by the strength of nationalism to unify cultures within borders while at the same time over-emphasizing cross-border distinctions. Whereas in the touristic town Guanajuato the burrito was threatened by the emerging popularity of the taco achieving a form of gastronomic hegemony in the first half of the twentieth century, in other parts of Mexico such as Sonora or in Baja California, the burrito remained by taking on a new and differentiated identity wrapped in a soft, wheat flour tortilla. Throughout the United States, the propagation of Mexican American food out of Los Angeles established in the American vocabulary what had been typically local terms: "burrito" and "soft-" and "hard tacos." In Mexico, this kind of industrial image of Mexican food created by immigrants and food processing was virtually unknown. However, the new fashion of Mexican American cuisine was not entirely

---

16. Smith, "Tacos, Enchiladas and Refried Beans," 7–8.
17. Pilcher, *Planet Taco,* 150–51.

estranged from authentic Mexican home cooking. By the 1970s, Mexican American cuisine had gained a nation-wide reputation beyond the Mexican community. But with a new generation of immigrants bringing their own regional cuisines in the 1980s, the standardization of the Mexican American cuisine faded away.[18]

Struggle, Cultural Differentiation, and Culinary Amalgamation

Like most of the food, the best way to enjoy tacos is when they are freshly prepared. Although the United States is strongly connected with fast food, and this kind of ready-to-eat business model can be found in most of the major urban centers, fast food in the United States is not excessively fast as global street cuisine fans can confirm. In Los Angeles, there are a large number of street vendors selling tacos, burritos, enchiladas and tortillas who are able to prepare appropriate dishes as quickly as any chain restaurant.[19]

However, there is a struggle between street vendors and restaurants as well as neighbors who consider the street vendors and taco truck operators a nuisance. Even if they are owned by Mexican Americans, their public presence made them vulnerable targets for anti-immigrant outrage. Fazila Bhimji has written on the undocumented Latino women and their experiences selling food on the streets of Los Angeles. She describes street vending as a form of survival strategy by often poorly educated and indigent immigrants lacking of skills, which makes it difficult for them to work in a formal setting. Being pushed into the informal sector, the mostly undocumented women don't have the resources to face the level of bureaucracy and expenses that street vending with permission could potentially involve. Thus, many of them remain without a license, are not allowed to sell their products lawfully, and made even more vulnerable in a sector confronted with rising competition.

---

18. Pilcher, *Planet Taco* 158–59.
19. Pilcher, *Planet Taco*, 4.

In several neighborhoods of Los Angeles, street vending has increased and gained in popularity among the mainstream population. While in earlier times selling food from carts was more common among the poorer immigrants, street food vending has now become a highly fashioned phenomenon. Los Angeles foodies started to follow their favorite food trucks on social media like Facebook or Twitter, discovering the advantage of saving money because it is cheaper than a restaurant and simultaneously enjoying the culinary experience of eating diverse foods from different countries. Driving around the city, one can observe various lines of people waiting for their meals bought on the street. Nevertheless, this kind of "hype" should not obscure the fact that street vending is a harsh business. Within it, there are notable differences and there is a hierarchy among the vendors. At the top are what have come to be known as gourmet food trucks, fully licensed and with rights to run in designated areas of the city. In the middle we find the traditional *loncheras* (food trucks), operated and managed usually by Latino immigrant families. Though they are licensed, many face financial struggles because of the city's ever changing regulations. On the bottom, finally, there are the street food vendors who sell from their carts with the least rights to city spaces and are considered among the poorest in terms of social class, though it seems that they are facing a growing acceptance in the mainstream.[20]

Clair M. Weber dedicated one of her articles to the undocumented Latino street vendors, which became a political issue in the late 1980s, when their number increased dramatically. Due to the rising immigration from Central America and Mexico at that time, many Latino women and men had been forced to work

---

20. Fazila Bhimji, "Struggles, Urban Citizenship, and Belonging: The Experience of Undocumented Street Vendors and Food Truck Owners in Los Angeles," *Urban Anthropology and Studies of Cultural Systems and World Economic Development* 39, no. 4 (Winter 2010), 470, http://www.jstor.org/stable/41291334.

in the informal economy.[21] In the battle of street vending it becomes obvious how the pursuit of culinary authenticity is tied to the complex connection between race and class. Initially, the consumers of the taco trucks, to a large extent, were the Latino lower classes, but in recent times it seems apparent that the trucks increasingly attract Anglos who search for exoticism and, of course, affordable meals.[22] Through their request of exotic food as well as their conviction in knowing what truly is authentic, today's taco truck followers appropriate a measure of cultural differentiation.

In Los Angeles, like elsewhere in the United States, within the Mexican American community, there are various culinary traditions that undergo fast-paced alteration. For a long time, tourism attracting mainstream Americans had been financially persisting for the Mexican cookery. However, Americanized foods are only distant reflections of Mexican food consisting of flavors that do not catch on with the Americans. Since Mexican American cooks have removed unpopular components and ingredients and instead substituted more agreeable flavors to cater to their American buyers, the Mexican American cuisine has little to do with the cuisine of Mexico. Rather, it is new types of cuisine, created out of a mixture of imported and also invented traditions—something that arose from the adjustment to local eating habits. But if Mexican food transformed too drastically in order to fit within the American palate, it would lose its roots. Such is a common fear; first and foremost, due to the culinary atrophy of becoming a mass-produced, fast food product.

---

21. Clair M. Weber, "Latino Street Vendors in Los Angeles: Heterogeneous Alliances, Community-Based Activism, and the State." *Asian and Latino Immigrants in A Restructuring Economy: The Metamorphosis of Southern California,* (Stanford: Stanford University Press, 2001), 219.

22. The term "Anglo" refers to the historic distinction between English and Spanish speakers in the Americas—particularly in the American Southwest during the westward expansion of the United States in the nineteenth century. The contemporary usage still denotes English-speakers but also infers that the "Anglo" is a white, non-Latino person.

Mexican foods in production, originally, were time-consuming, laborious, and costly. Its commercialization required easier, cheaper and faster production methods. In this way, Mexican food lost its soul; the intense involvement of unique techniques known to the traditional cook had been abandoned. Nevertheless, not all is lost; among Anglo-Americans a new awareness and sophisticated palate has arisen which stems from the current attention towards the resurgence of Mexican cuisine. In the city, there is a wealth of street vendors, many of them with Mexican origins, who emphasize their culinary particularities in the food they are selling on the street. Locally and directly prepared on site by hand with fresh ingredients they try their best to defy restaurants and fast food chains.[23]

Besides the fusion of the Mexican and American cuisine, there are also other types of culinary amalgamations, like the example of the Kogi trucks. In 2008, Kogi gained local, and later national, fame by selling a surprisingly successful blend of Korean and Mexican food. One of the most famous dishes became soy-marinated short rib tacos with coriander and cabbage which has since been adopted by many others. Name any cuisine and one will see that by now, someone in the city has tried to put it in or on a tortilla. It seems that in Los Angeles, where Latinos make up the single largest ethnic group, Mexican cuisine is the base upon which the reinterpretation of other food habits is built. While Ara's Tacos offers Armenian-styled grilled meat spit merged with tacos, White Rabbit Truck prepares Filipino chicken, sausage, and chopped, fried pork with tacos, and El Sushi Loco serves Mexicanized sushi rolls. To know the exact location of the Kogi trucks customers can follow their routes via twitter, where Kogi has 96,000 followers. Aside from the hype on social media, its head chef, Roy Choi, was named best new chef in the United States by *Food & Wine* magazine; quite an honor if one considers that his kitchen has to fit into a van or trailer.[24]

---

23. Smith, "Tacos, Enchiladas and Refried Beans," 12.

24. Rebecca Seal, "Mexican Street Food in Los Angeles." *The Observer* (US Edition), May 26, 2012, http://www.theguardian.com/travel/2012/may/27/mexicostreet-food-los-angeles.

In Los Angeles, it is possible to eat a range of inexpensive, delicious, single-culture cuisines, but the aforementioned reinterpretation is a shift in food culture. This shift spread as cooks at cafés, restaurants, and food trucks try out something new, something that mirrors the creativity in Los Angeles. Many people call it fusion cuisine, partially because of the absence of a well-defined vocabulary for the multiethnic mixing occurring on the Los Angeles food scene. Historically, fusion contains the reformulation of ethnic cuisine to make it more suitable for rich, white customers. This was the case and can be still, though not exclusively, as the Filipino restaurateur Oscar Bautista, born and living in Los Angeles says: "There's really no fusion about it. When it comes down to it, all of us here, we're American to the bone. These are the flavors we grew up with."[25] But there are also divergent opinions on the subject like another newspaper article shows.

Carolina Miranda, a journalist in Southern California, writes in her review on Gustavo Arellano's book *Taco USA. How Mexican Food Conquered America* that almost all of the tacos the Americans eat are the very same—a fusion. Although the recipes have their roots in Mexico, the scale and presentation is all American. Tacos have become so American that sometimes they barely seem Mexican any more.[26] However, it would be wrong to think about the sociopolitical future of the city as an all-you-can-eat buffet of multicultural experiences. This fusion of culinary cultures does not need a corresponding resolution of current problems such as unemployment, poverty, educational inequity, and racism. The exciting food culture in Los Angeles with its

25. Julianne Hing, "L.A. Food Culture Offers A Glimpse into 'The New America.'" *ColorLines*, April 26, 2013, http://colorlines.com/archives/2013/04/in_los_angeles_multiethnic_food_culture_offers_a_taste_of_the_new_america.html.

26. Carolina Miranda, "The California Taco Trail: How Mexican Food Conquered America." *National Public Radio Washington, D.C.*, April 23, 2012, http://www.npr.org/blogs/thesalt/2012/04/23/150886690/the-california-taco-trail-how-mexican-food-conquered-america.

multiethnic food offerings is not necessarily a measure for deeper multiracial bonds. Like in art, fashion, or music, the food habits of people of color are a hot commodity and food is culture; but culture also is a tough business.[27]

Conclusion: Adjustment, Mixture, or Fusion?

In this essay, the goal was to analyze the relationship between Mexican and American cuisine. One way of how Mexican cookery became significant in the American cuisine was through immigrant Mexican farm workers who brought their food habits with them when moving to the United States. Glen Bell strongly contributed to commercialization by launching his taco-empire. However, Mexican immigrants had a great share in this development, because in fact, it was the Mexican Americans who invented the iconic American-styled taco by adapting one of their foods to a changing society as a mutual part of divided local cuisines. Over time, more and more elements of the former Mexican cuisine found their expression in the Anglo-American way of eating, and in order to address a greater amount of people in the United States, Mexican foods were transformed to align with American food habits. But through its conformation, more and more Mexicans began to deny its recognition as Mexican. One reason could be that the Mexican cuisine in the United States is only a distant reflection of the Mexican food consisting of flavors that do not catch on with Americans. The same happened with the taco when it became a mass-produced, fast-food product. But among Anglo-Americans, new awareness and a sophisticated palate has brought current attention to the Mexican cuisine. My aim was to determine whether there was an adjustment of the imported food traditions of the Mexicans to the local food habits of Los Angeles, and I have come to the conclusion that this would only be an

27. Hing, "L.A. Food Culture."

over-simplification. Rather than a mere adjustment, new types of food evolved— the result of a mixture of imported traditions from the Mexican immigrants and something that arose from the adaption to local eating habits of the United States. At the end it emerges that this is a question that really can not be answered in an appropriate way. In the colorful world of tastes, there exits far more diversity, which is beyond any clear distinction and attribution of ethnicity and cultural incorporation. As a result of this examination, it appears that besides the fusion of the Mexican and American way of eating, there is a variety of gastronomic differentiation and culinary amalgamation within it. However, what the Mexican American cuisine and hence the Americanized taco mirror–adjustment, fusion, mixture or something totally divergent–finally remains a matter of own sensation and arises from everyone's very personal perception.

Bibliography

Appadurai, Arjun. *Modernity at Large: Cultural Dimension of Globalization*. Minneapolis: University of Minnesota Press, 1996.

Arellano, Gustavo. *Taco USA: How Mexican Food Conquered America*. New York: Scribner, 2013.

Bhimji, Fazila. "Struggles, Urban Citizenship, and Belonging: The Experience of Undocumented Street Vendors and Food Truck Owners in Los Angeles." *Urban Anthropology and Studies of Cultural Systems and World Economic Development* 39, no. 4 (Winter 2010): 455–92. http://www.jstor.org/stable/41291334.

Hing, Julianne. "L.A. Food Culture Offers A Glimpse into 'The New America.'" *ColorLines*, April 26, 2013. http://colorlines.com/archives/2013/04/in_los_angeles_multiethnic_food_culture_offers_a_taste_of_the_new_america.html.

Miranda, Carolina. "The California Taco Trail: How Mexican Food Conquered America." *National Public Radio Washington, D.C.*, April 23, 2012. http://www.npr.org/blogs/thesalt/2012/04/23/150886690/the-california-taco-trail-howmexican-food-conquered-america.

Pilcher, Jeffrey M. *Planet Taco: A Global History of the Mexican Food*. New York: Oxford University Press, 2012.

Seal, Rebecca. "Mexican Street Food in Los Angeles." *The Observer*, May 27, 2012. http://www.theguardian.com/travel/2012/may/27/mexicostreet-food-los-angeles.

Smith, Andrew. "Tacos, Enchiladas and Refried Beans: The Invention of Mexican-American Cookery." Presentation at "Cultural and Historical Aspects of Foods - Yesterday, Today, and Tomorrow," symposium at Oregon State University, April 9–11, 1999. http://web.archive.org/web/20070404220418/http://food.oregonstate.edu/ref/culture/mexico_smith.html.

Valle, Victor M., and Rodolfo D. Torres. *Latino Metropolis.* Globalization and Community 7. Minneapolis: University of Minnesota, 2000.

Vélez-Ibáñez, Carlos G. *Border Visions: Mexican Cultures of the Southwest United States.* Tucson: The University of Arizona Press, 1996.

Wallendorf, Melanie, and Michael D. Reilly. "Ethnic Migration, Assimilation, and Consumption." *Journal of Consumer Research* 10, no. 3 (Winter 1983), 292–302. http://www.jstor.org/stable/2488801.

Weber, Clair M. "Latino Street Vendors in Los Angeles: Heterogeneous Alliances, Community-Based Activism, and the State." *Asian and Latino Immigrants in a Restructuring Economy: The Metamorphosis of Southern California,* 217–40. Stanford: Stanford University Press, 2001.

The Death of the Würstelstand: Turkish Migration and Austrian Resistance as Seen through the Microcosm of Street Food in Vienna's Twentieth District

Rachel Kaye

On September 12, 1983, a plaque was placed on the Leopoldsberg in Vienna. This plaque memorializes the 300th anniversary of the Battle of Vienna. In 1683, the citizens of Vienna came together in a heroic effort to turn back the forces of the Ottoman Empire. This Austrian victory marked a turning-point for the Habsburg Empire in their over-300-year struggle against the Ottoman Empire.

When one visits the picturesque Vienna today, the story is not one of sieges and battles but one of seeming co-existence and hybridization. Beside the glistening shores of the Danube one sees families of mixed heritage, picnicking and grilling next to one another in a seemingly peaceful culmination of cultures. Yet the question remains: How has Turkish migration been received by the Austrian residents of Vienna? Is it really a relationship of hybridization and acceptance; or is there more to this partnership than meets the eye?

This article examines the effects of Turkish migration through the lens of street food culture. Using statistics, supplied by the Wirtschaftskammer Österreich (WKÖ) and Statistik Österreich, I will establish the correlation between Turkish migration starting in the 1960s and the influx of Kebab stands in a market traditionally dominated by Würstelstände. Once this adaptation in the traditional street food market of Vienna is accepted, one can begin to look at how this change has been received by Viennese citizens.

Focusing on Vienna's Twentieth District, Brigittenau, this article examines street food culture in Vienna, including the rise, and supposed fall, of the Würstelstand.[1] Furthermore, through newspaper articles, secondary sources, and a survey of residents, this article discusses links between migration, assimilation, intolerance, and rebellion, using the microcosm of street food culture.

This interaction is particularly enticing for me as I both work part-time in a Turkish-themed restaurant, which sells both Kebab and Würstl, and live in the Twentieth District of Vienna. The population of the Twentieth District has the largest percentage of Turkish immigrants in all of Vienna.[2] My close proximity with both the regulars of the restaurant, and the restaurant's mixed Turkish and Austrian owners, partially inspired this specific case study. Additionally, although my background is in Global History, I find Austrian history particularly intriguing. The idea of a specific Austrian identity has been a re-occurring theme in my research efforts. The closeness to my field of expertise, in combination with my own personal desire to understand what it means to be Austrian, has led me to this project.

This project provides a springboard for further research. A larger study could extend this approach from the Twentieth District to the whole of Vienna. One could also focus on Turkish interpretations of migrating to Austria rather than on how Austrians relate to Turkish migration. This project is important as it allows for more insight into the idea of what it means to be Viennese in a modern society. As someone interested in identity studies, it is imperative that I understand my subjects, not only in a historical sense but also in an anthropological sense.

---

1. Erich Kocina, "Kebab-Hype: Wien zieht Bremse," *Die Presse*, January 15, 2010, http://diepresse.com/home/panorama/wien/533222/KebabHype; and Florian Kobler, "Würstelstände leiden unter Konkurrenz," *Orf*, March 2, 2014, http://wien.orf.at/news/stories/2577809/.

2. Rita Schneider-Sliwa, ed., *Cities in Transition: Globalization, Political Change and Urban Development*, GeoJournal Library 83 (Dordrecht, Netherlands: Springer, 2006), 217.

There are existing studies which look at the details of immigration and migrant workers including the series volume *Cities in Transition Globalization, Political Change and Urban Development*. While such an article provides important statistics, it fails to discuss why Turkish workers are segregated to certain parts of the city or market. Similar articles such as Maren Möhring's "Transnational Food Migration and the Internalization of Food Consumption: Ethnic Cuisine in West Germany," have addressed trends in Berlin but I was unable to find an academic study linking Turkish migration and street food culture in Vienna.[3]

Using aspects from Edward Said's idea of the "Other," which is "a style of thought based upon an ontological and epistemological distinction made between "the Orient" and (most of the time) "the Occident," I argue that Austrian politics have been flavored with an othering of the Turkish community since the start of the late twentieth century.[4] This is not a complete Orientalizing in the sense of Edward Said, but rather a surface othering which has happened in the last fifty years. One cannot really apply orientalism in a historic or geographic sense as Turkey was seen as a part of Europe. These aspects are carried down through newspapers and radio, and influence how some residents of the Twentieth District think about their Turkish neighbors. Using newspaper articles and various statements from politicians, this article demonstrates that a dialogue of "otherness" is used to portray members of various foreign communities. By contrasting Turkish community members to an Austrian norm, particular media outlets have influenced not only the way residents think, but also the way they vote, eat, and—importantly for this article—the way they think about street food consumption and economics. Furthermore, this article argues

---

3. Maren Möhring, "Transnational Food Migration and the Internalization of Food Consumption: Ethnic Cuisine in West Germany," in *Food and Globalization: Consumption, Markets and Politics in the Modern World*, ed. Alexander Nützenadel and Frank Trentmann (Oxford: Berg, 2008)

4. Edward Said, *Orientalism*, (London: Penguin Books, 1977), 1–3.

that due to this dialogue of othering, hybridization as expressed by Arjun Appadurai cannot be fully achieved because "according to the hybridization view, external and internal flows interact to create a unique cultural hybrid that encompasses components of the two."[5] In short, "the main thesis of cultural hybridization is the continuous process of mixing or blending cultures."[6] This lack of hybridization in combination with the "othering" of the Turkish community, has led instead to a fear that the rise of the Kebab symbolizes the death of Austrian culture and in the sense of the food community, the death of the Würstelstand.

Austria and the Würstelstand: "Es ist mir Wurst!"

After many years of interaction between the Habsburg and Ottoman Empires, Turkish migration intensified in the 1960s with the creation of the *Gastarbeiter* program. This program will be discussed in a later section in more detail, and for even more information one should read Heinz Kriz's article, "Hidden Comeback," which appears in this edited volume. It is clear that the Gastarbeiter program, despite its original purpose, began a process of continuous immigration. With this migration, the Turkish people have brought with them their own unique food culture, which has transformed the street food markets of Vienna and has disquieted many of those surveyed; however, before one can look at the changes in the Viennese street food market one must have an understanding of what comprises traditional Viennese street food.

Leonhard Weidinger writes, "Internationally, the Wiener is probably one of the most famous culinary ambassadors of the

---

5. Abderrahman Hassi and Giovanna Storti, "Globalization and Culture: The Three H Scenarios," in *Globalization – Approaches to Diversity*, ed. Hector Cuadra-Montiel (Intech, 2012), doi: 10.5772/45655.
6. Hassi and Storti, "Globalization and Culture."

city, along with the Schnitzel and the Sachertorte."[7] The Frankfurter, known outside of Vienna as the Wienerwurst, and the Würstelstand have become integral symbols of Austrian culture. The Würstelstand is a place where lawyers and laymen, doctors and deliverymen all meet with the purpose of a quick bite to eat and perhaps to share a story or beer. On the one hand orders such as "a Eitrige mit an Bugl, an Schoafn und a Hüsn" [lit. a pus-filled one with a hump, hot spice, and a tube]" (a polish cheese kransky with a roll, spicy mustard, and a beer) or "a Haaße aufgschnitn mit an Siaßn und an Scheazl, und a Sechzehnablech dazu [lit. a hot one, sliced with a sweet and a heel, and a no.16 tin with it]" (a Waldviertler sausage, sliced with sweet mustard and a heel of bread, and a can of Ottakringer beer) have become Vienna cult classics, to the point of cliché; but on the other hand, the Würstelstand is a relatively recent development.[8]

Sebastian Hackenschmidt explains, "Street food culture developed only in the course of industrialization—particularly in the larger cities—due to the change to factory production and the concomitant longer work commutes and shorter breaks." From the nineteenth century until the early twentieth the sausages were sold in movable street carts that were dragged to various locations. "Fixed locations were not established until the 1960s, when permanent stands—which are now part of the overall image of the city—were officially permitted in Vienna."[9] Yet, the idea of the Wurst as a trademark of Austrian culture resonates deeper than simply the physical stands. "Es ist mir wurscht" means to the Viennese "it doesn't matter to me," "Wurstigkeit" is a synonym for indifference or lack of interest.[10] These phrases can be heard over-

---

7. Sebastian Hackenschmidt, *Fünf und Neunzig Wiener Würstel Stände: The hot 95* (Vienna: Verlag Anton Pustet, 2013), 140.

8. Hackenschmidt, *Fünf und Neunzig*, 8.

9. Hackenschmidt, *Fünf und Neunzig*, 16.

10. Hackenschmidt, *Fünf und Neunzig*, 140.

all in Austria, not only in Vienna, but from the remotest parts of Lower Austria to Upper Austria and Tirol. In 2014, Austria even won the Eurovision Song Contest, with a contestant named Conchita Wurst. Conchita chose this name because she believed that the prejudices against homo- and transsexuals were "Wurst," or in other words not even worthy of discussion.

So what does this recently invented Austrian tradition say about its people? After the Second World War, Austrian's sought to distance themselves from the Germans and the other Axis Powers. Therefore, in October 1943, during the Moscow Declaration on Austria when it was claimed that Austria had been the "first victim of Hitler's aggression,"[11] Austrian statesmen took this opportunity to distance themselves from the aggressor nations of the Second World War. In this process they sought points of pride in Austrian culture. Mozart, who was not technically born in Austria, Sisi, and many of the Habsburg relics were brought to the forefront as cultural symbols of Austrian separateness. Austria's Second Republic made use of an extremely long and rich Austrian history. This idea became known as the "Ostarrichi myth."[12] The word Ostarrichi is the middle-high German word for Austria. "It was first mentioned in AD 996 documenting Leopold of Babenberg's lands along the Danube in today's Lower Austria."[13] Evoking this idea of an ancient Austria helped root the nation in the Middle Ages. This Heimat Austria is a one-thousand-year-old country with a wealth of history, full of cultural traditions and picturesque landscapes.

With this history, politicians were able to denote a clear cultural identity, which was different from that of Germany. Linking the Second Republic with the Habsburg Empire replaced "the myth

---

11. G. R. Knight, "Contours of Memory in Post-Nazi Austria," *Patterns of Prejudice* 34, no. 4 (2000), 3.

12. Margarete Lamb-Faffelberger, "Beyond the Sound of Music: The Quest for Cultural Identity in Modern Austria," *The German Quarterly* 76, no. 3 (2003), 290.

13. Lamb-Faffelberger, "Beyond the Sound of Music," 290.

of Austrians as the better Germans which was prevalent during the years of the destitute First Republic (1918-38)."[14] This differentiation reinforced the idea that the Austrians "suffered occupation and were liberated after the devastating war."[15] In a similar vein, Austrian culinary tradition sought to differentiate itself from its German neighbors. Austrian's perfected the art of making sausages and claimed it as their own badge of Austrian culture. With the importance of the Wurst in mind, one must now turn to another key event of the 1960s, more specifically the Gastarbeiter program.

1960s Turkish Immigration into Austria—Where They Live and What They Do

Foreigners in Vienna can be divided according to "nationality, or according to the social prestige given by the local population."[16] According to Andrea Kampschulte, "the social acceptance of the migrants is very different."[17] More specifically she explains that a small group of respected and well-educated foreigners of mostly Western origin stands out against a large, low-educated and often discriminated group of temporary laborers. The Turkish population in Vienna falls mainly into this population known in German as "GastarbeiterInnen."

During the Gastarbeiter programs of the 1960s and early 1970s, the Austrian government recruited temporary labor migrants for low-skilled jobs. These migrants came mainly from rural areas in less developed countries, especially Turkey and former Yugoslavia. The Gastarbeiter program was based on the premise that immigrant workers would return to their country of origin after working abroad for a certain amount of time. Consequently, there

---

14. Lamb-Faffelberger, "Beyond the Sound of Music," 291.
15. Lamb-Faffelberger, "Beyond the Sound of Music," 293.
16. Schneider-Sliwa, *Cities in Transition*, 207.
17. Schneider-Sliwa, *Cities in Transition*, 207.

were no policies aimed at improving the educational and qualification level of these immigrants and their children and their integration into Austrian society.[18] "On the contrary, there were legal impediments to the integration of immigrants into society, such as curtailed rights and obstacles to the acquisition of permanent resident status and citizenship."[19] Revealingly, immigrant children were often offered language courses in their native languages, rather than in German, in an attempt to ease re-integration into the country of origin of their parents. These GastarbeiterInnen and their families were seen and treated as separate entities from Austrian natives, as "others," who were temporarily in Austria to work the undesirable jobs before heading back to their homelands.

Austrian statistics reveal that whereas only 25,909 residents with migration backgrounds lived in Vienna in 1961, the figure had increased to 113,423 by 1981 accounting for 7.4 percent of the total population. In 1993, about a quarter of the residential population of Vienna consisted of foreigners.[20]

With the influx of Turkish GastarbeiterInnen coming to Vienna, separate residential areas began to form. Turkish areas were established in the Tenth and Twentieth Districts where residents with Turkish roots currently account for 24.5 percent and 25.8 percent respectively, of residents with migration backgrounds in these districts.[21] This separation in the housing districts, in addition to segregation in the labor market, has led to an even more pronounced ethnic separatism and an "othering" of all things

---

18. Julia Mourão Permoser and Sieglinde Rosenberger, "Integration Policy in Austria," in *International Perspectives: Integration and Inclusion*, ed. J. Frideres and J. Biles. Queen's Policy Studies Series (Montreal: McGill-Queen's University Press, 2012), 41. http://politikwissenschaft.univie.ac.at/fileadmin/user_upload/inst_politikwiss/Permoser/publications/7_Mourao_Permoser_Rosenberger_2012_Integration_Policy_in_Austria_in_Biles_Friederes.pdf.
19. Mourão Permoser and Rosenberger, "Integration Policy in Austria," 41.
20. Schneider-Sliwa, *Cities in Transition*, 217.
21. Schneider-Sliwa, *Cities in Transition*, 220.

Turkish. This distinction in employment can be seen in various immigrant groups. Turks, for example, "work predominantly as traders and dealers in the public food markets."[22] What started as a means to feed the Turkish *GastarbeiterInnen* has evolved into a larger market. Select owners (mainly also with Turkish origin) have started selling Döner Kebab which was a Berlin invention from the 1960s. This street food was created when the Turkish immigrants to Germany took a traditional meat and bread and combined them into something completely new. This invention spread throughout Europe. With the flow of Turkish immigrants to Austria one can see the start of Kebab stands popping up around the Twentieth District, as well as the rest of Vienna.

Like the Second Republic in Austria, Turkey as a nation state was created during the twentieth century. Furthermore, like Austria, it is a complicated matter to talk about a uniform Turkish identity. Before one can attempt to do this, one must look at what is meant by the rise of the nation state and subsequently what it means to have a national identity.

In 1983, Benedict Anderson introduced the term "Imagined Community" and explained its role in the rise of the nation state. Anderson states that a nation is a form of artificial structure. He explains that it "is imagined because the members of even the smallest nation will never know most of their fellow-members, meet them, or even hear of them, yet in the minds of each lives the image of their communion."[23] This sort of grouping is taken for granted as a systematic way of looking at the world. Yet the rise of the so-called nation state is a comparatively recent development. Part of the creation of the nation state involved the formulation of a national identity: a collective past defined through specific historic moments, leaders, heroes, cuisine, and music. Shared

---

22. Schneider-Sliwa, *Cities in Transition*, 225.

23. Benedict R. Anderson, *Imagined Communities: Reflections on the Origin and Spread of Nationalism* (London: Verso, 1991), 224.

experiences were collected and amalgamated into an identity; this process of constructing a certain past for the sake of a common identity is also called "the invention of tradition" and was coined by Eric Hobsbawm and Terence Ranger.[24]

Prior to kingdoms and the conception of the nation state there were various groups of peoples bound together through common ancestry and history, yet there was no geographical border in which this process was limited. The creation of specific borders and the acknowledgment of common history within these constricted regions led to the development of a homogenous example of a region's culture that each citizen should attempt to assimilate. This adjusted the idea of culture and with it the ideas about a shared history. National pride helps to define what it means to be a member of a nation state. When talking about the Turkish nation state it is very difficult to find this homogenous identity. There is, however, a relatively large population of Turkish individuals who practice the Islamic religion. This religion has in many ways helped to define the modern Turkish nation state, and many of the resentments, as is later made clear through a survey of Austrian residents of the Twentieth District as well as select newspaper articles, seem to be pointed at this aspect of Turkish identity.

Reactions to Turkish Immigration and the Rise of the Döner Kebab

According to one article from the Austrian newspaper, *Der Standard*, tensions surrounding Turkish migration are sometimes showcased at street food stands. Würstelstand owner Frau Waltraud states, "*Ich mag's net, die sollen daham bleiben*" (I don't like them, they should stay home). Waltraud furthers that, "die meisten Tür-

---

24. Eric Hobsbawn, "Introduction: Inventing Traditions," in *The Invention of Tradition*, ed. Eric Hobswbawn and Terence Ranger (Cambridge: Cambridge University Press, 1992), 1.

ken ein G'sindel sind" (most Turks are riff-raff). [25] In the same article, the mayor of Waldegg, Johann Kleslis—a member of the *Sozialdemokratische Partei Österreichs* (SPÖ)— went on record stating that the integration problems are not due to the people of his jurisdiction, but rather due to the mentality of the Turkish people. Another Austrian newspaper, *Die Presse*, explains that the competition between the Kebab stand and the Würstelstand is reaching a critical point. The article further asserts that one increasingly hears the Austrian people complaining that the Turkish fast food stands are gaining the upper hand.[26]. In a similar vein, an article from the *Freiheitliche Partei Österreichs* (FPÖ) warns that the good, old Würstelstände in cities like Vienna, Linz, and Graz are threatened with extinction.[27] In Hackenschmidt's work on the Vienna Würstelstände, he explains that in conservative circles it is often stated that the real Vienna Würstelstand is dying out, to more exotic foods such as Döner, gyros, pizza, hamburgers, and falafel.[28]

There are however, other opinions that are not nearly so bleak. Josef Bitzinger, the vice-president for the Vienna tourism association, chairman of the Vienna Chamber of Commerce, and owner of a few successful classic Würstelstände, explains that there is no reason to worry about the Würstelstand. He believes that there will always be Würstelstände in Vienna.[29] Erich Kocina writes for *Die Presse* that, in pure numbers, the picture is not as dramatic as it is often portrayed. He explains the statistics state that there are 157 Würstelstände, in comparison with 106 kiosks

---

25. Lukas Kapeller, "Die wollen sich nicht anfreunden," *Der Standard*, July 3, 2008, http://derstandard.at/3045637/Lokalaugenschein-Die-wollen-sich-nicht-anfreunden#.

26. Kocina, "Kebab-Hype," *Die Presse*.

27. "Heimische Wirtshauskultur wird von Kebab & Co. Verdrängt," *Unzensuriert.at*, February 3, 2013, http://www.unzensuriert.at/content/0011590-Heimische-Wirtshauskultur-wird-von-Kebab-Co-verdr-ngt.

28. Hackenschmidt, *Fünf und Neunzig*, 9.

29. Kocina, "Kebab-Hype," *Die Presse*.

that were listed as other. The category of "*sonstiges*" (other) in-cludes kebab, pizza, and Indian products. Yet, it is hard to say ex-actly how many Würstelstände there are in Vienna, the Austrian Chamber of Commerce (WKÖ) lists 441 stands, however, Kebab stands are also included in these numbers, making things more difficult.[30] Additionally, if someone owns more than one stand he is only registered once. It is however clear that Vienna is still far away from a crisis, as the classic Würstelstände are well visited. Alexander Hengl, the food inspector for the stands acknowledges that stereotypes exist about the cleanliness of Kebab stands, but he argues that these accusations are unfounded. He even states that sometimes Würstelstände are not as clean as the Kebab stands. For these reasons, Kocina's assertion that the rotating meat skew-er, which looks like a minaret (a symbol of foreignness), could be an object behind which "the fear of immigrants" is hidden, not only possible, but downright logical.[31]

A Small Study of the Twentieth District

Relying on newspapers does not replace empirical research, and therefore, I conducted a survey of forty residents of the Twen-tieth District in order to gather information about their opinions on kebab, Turkish migration, and the idea of the possible death of the Würstelstand. The survey struggled to find balance in its participants as 73 percent of those surveyed were men, and all but two of those surveyed were thirty years or older. Yet, despite its shortcomings, some of the results were particularly telling. For example, 64 percent of those surveyed believed that the Würstel-stand's existence is threatened by the introduction of the Kebab Stand. Additionally, 50 percent eat kebab a few times a year and

---

30. Florian Kobler, "Würstelstände leiden unter Konkurrenz," *ORF*, March 2, 2014, http://wien.orf.at/news/stories/2626399/.
31. Kocina, "Kebab-Hype", *Die Presse*.

24 percent never eat kebab. On the other hand, only two people surveyed never eat Würstl and 39 percent eat Würstl monthly or more. Most of those surveyed stated that they have no political party. Seven out of forty aligned themselves with SPÖ, three with FPÖ, two with the Green Party, and two with *Das Neue Österreich und Liberales Forum*. From the responses, 61 percent believed that adding specialties other than Würstl to the stands was a bad idea and a few responses explained that this was not good due to health reasons and decaying standards. Those that did in fact find the integration acceptable, praised the idea of a larger selection and wrote that when the product (Würstel) is good, than there is no reason to fear its extinction. The most noteworthy point in the survey, however, regarded the Islamic religion.

Interestingly, thirteen from the forty people surveyed, wrote in the open response section, some sort of reference to the Islam as a deciding factor in whether or not one is ready to integrate to Austrian society. This idea is not only controversial, but also extremely complicated. The idea of Islam as a deterrent to integration is discussed by Julia Mourão Permoser and Sieglinde Rosenberger in their chapter on integration policy in Austria. They explain: "The allegation that certain communities are not well integrated is also often brought up in connection with religion, especially Islam."[32] Although Austria has an inclusive model of religious governance, which allows multiple recognized official religions, Muslims are often nevertheless targeted with rhetoric, which stresses that they do not conform to the Austrian political and educational systems. They are especially chastised in respects to gender equality. In the Interior Ministry of Austria's commissioned report about Muslims in Austria, known as "the integration study," authors reached the conclusion that there was, "a significantly large group of Muslims who were very religiously observant and conservative in their opinions. These were deemed

---

32. Mourão Permoser and Rosenberger, "Integration Policy in Austria," 46.

to be 'unwilling to integrate.'"[33] With this in mind, it seems relatively plausible to conclude that the animosity against Kebab stands has little to do with the actual food but rather expresses a larger fear of the "other" and the hybridization, or the dilution, of Austrian culture in the wake of migration.

Conclusion

Through my research, it became clear that the classic Würstelstand is not endangered as many newspaper articles describe. There are, nevertheless, problems in the interaction between Turkish immigrants and previous *GastarbeiterInnen* and Austrian natives in Vienna. Cultural and culinary differences, strengthened by segregation in education, housing, and the labor market, have combined with an "othering" of Turkish culture and customs to create an atmosphere of animosity instead of hybridization. It is not clear whether Turkish immigrants are "unwilling to integrate" or whether Austrian locals have segregated immigrants to the point where it is extremely difficult to assimilate; however, it seems clear that these tensions are mirrored in arguments surrounding the Würstelstand in comparison with Kebab stands.[34] It is furthermore true that as more peoples migrate to Austria, and specifically to Vienna, a larger selection of food is offered on the street. Many stands have adapted to the various clientele, that visit them, but this has not, as many seem to believe, led to the loss of classic Würstelstände. On the contrary, the street food market continues to thrive in Vienna.

---

33. Permoser and Rosenberger, "Integration Policy in Austria," 46–47.
34. Permoser and Rosenberger, "Integration Policy in Austria," 46–47.

Bibliography

Appadurai, Arjun. *Modernity at Large: Cultural Dimensions of Globalization.* Public Worlds 1. Minneapolis: University of Minnesota Press, 2010.

Anderson, Benedict R. *Imagined communities: Reflections on the Origin and Spread of Nationalism.* London: Verso, 1991.

Ashcroft, Bill, Gareth Griffiths, and Helen Tiffen. "Re-Placing Theory: Post-Colonial Writing and Literary Theory." In *The Empire Writes Back: Theory and Practice in Post-Colonial Literatures.* 2nd ed. New York: Routledge, 2002. 153–92.

Borkert, Maren, Wolfgang Bosswick, Friderich Heckmann, and Doris Lüken-Klaßen. "Local integration policies for migrants in Europe." European Foundation for the Improvement of Living and Working Conditions. Bamberg, Germany: European Forum for Migration Studies, 2007.

Hackenschmidt Sebastian. *Fünf und Neunzig Wiener Würstel Stände: The Hot 95.* Vienna: Verlag Anton Pustet, 2013.

Hobsbawm, Eric. "Introduction: Inventing Traditions." In *The Invention of Tradition*, edited by Eric Hobsbawm and Terence Ranger, 1–14. Cambridge: Cambridge University Press, 1992.

Knight, G.R. "Contours of Memory in Post-Nazi Austria" *Patterns of Prejudice* 34, no. 4 (2000): 5-11

Möhring, Maren. "Transnational Food Migration and the Internalization of Food Consumption: Ethnic Cuisine in West Germany." In *Food and Globalization: Consumption, Markets and Politics in the Modern World*, edited by Alexander Nützenadel and Frank Trentmann, 129–50. Oxford: Berg, 2008.

Mourão Permoser, Julia, and Sieglinde Rosenberger. "Integration Policy in Austria." In *International Perspectives: Integration and Inclusion*, edited by J. Frideres and J. Biles, 39–58. Queen's Policy Studies Series. Montreal: McGill-Queen's University Press, 2012. http://politikwissenschaft.univie.ac.at/fileadmin/user_upload/inst_politikwiss/Permoser/publications/7_Mourao_Permoser_Rosenberger_2012_Integration_Policy_in_Austria_in_Biles_Friederes.pdf.

Said, Edward. *Orientalism*. London: Penguin Books, 1977.

Schneider, Rita. *Cities in Transition: Globalization, Political Change and Urban Development*. GeoJournal Library 83. Dordrecht, Netherlands: Springer, 2006.

Wirtschaftskammer Österreich website, http://www.wko.at.

Newspapers

Brugger, Magdalena. "Auf der Spuren der Türken." *Wiener Zeitung*, May 2014. http://www.wienerzeitung.at/themen_channel/integration/migration/629788_Auf-den-Spuren-derTuerken.html.

Kapeller, Lukas. "Die wollen sich nicht anfreunden" *Der Standard*, July 3, 2008. http://derstandard.at/3045637/Lokalaugenschein-Die-wollen-sich-nicht-anfreunden#.

Kocina, Erich. "Kebab-Hype: Wien zieht Bremse." *Die Presse*, January 15, 2010. http://diepresse.com/home/panorama/wien/533222/KebabHype_Wien-zieht-Bremse.

Kobler, Florian. "Würstelstände leiden unter Konkurrenz." *Orf*, March 2, 2014. http://wien.orf.at/news/stories/2577809/.

"Gekommen, um zu bleiben." *Wiener Zeitung*, May 12, 2014. http://www.wienerzeitung.at/themen_channel/integration/migration/?em_cnt=629522&em_cnt_page=2.

"Heimische Wirtshauskultur wird von Kebab & Co. Verdrängt." *FPÖ Zeitschrift*, February 3, 2013. http://www.unzensuriert.at/content/0011590-Heimische-Wirtshauskultur-wird-von-Kebab-Co-verdr-ngt.

Zeman, Barbara. "Wien am Spieß." *Falter*, February 28, 2006. http://www.falter.at/falter/2006/02/28/wien-am-spiess/.

Hidden Comeback:
The Impact of the Yugoslavian Guestworkers on Street Food Habits in Vienna

Heinz Kriz

Immigrants from Yugoslavia and Street Food Culture in Vienna

Migration movements in the twentieth century have had a significant impact on street food served in Vienna today as Rachel Kaye highlights, but are there particular influences before, during, or after the period of *Gastarbeiterpolitik*? What are the repercussions of decades of organized mass-migration? There was an evident change of Yugoslavian and Balkan-style street food in Vienna. It spread through the impact of the *GastarbeiterInnen* (guest workers) because of their changed mobility in society, which correlated to the migratory status of these people as well as the distribution of street food, and an urban society that emphasized mobility and efficiency?

This topic is relevant because the link between the street food habits of the so-called Yugoslavian GastarbeiterInnen and their impact on street food culture in Vienna has been overlooked in current research. Compared to the large percentage of Yugoslavians in the labor force during the period between 1970 and 1980 (between 73 percent and 80 percent of the foreign work force in Vienna) the influence of their food habits often seems to be undervalued because of the similarities between street food consumed in former Yugoslavia and in Austria.[1] It seems dubious that the largest group of GastarbeiterInnen in Vienna did not have any

1. Helga Leitner, *Gastarbeiter in der städtischen Gesellschaft: Segregation, Integration und Assimilation von Arbeitsmigranten. Am Beispiel jugoslawischer Gastarbeiter in Wien* (Frankfurt am Main: Campus, 1983), 27.

effect on the street food culture of the city. The goal of the following pages is to investigate the period from 1945, the end of World War II, which was characterized by the increasing importance of Austria as a transit country, until the end of the 1970s. This time frame includes the ban of recruitment 1974 and the phenomenon of families of the GastarbeiterInnen that followed them to Austria. Furthermore, this article addresses if there exists any evidence that this particular immigration movement influenced Viennese street food habits and in what way. To analyze and reconstruct the impact of the Yugoslavian immigrants on street food, it was methodologically essential to assemble sociological data and sources of the 1970s with recent literature of the field of immigration research.

The literature of the 1970s and 1980s related to GastarbeiterInnen focuses mainly on the housing situation, the daily racism in the host country, or the challenges of adequate support for children of GastarbeiterInnen in public schools. Since the beginning of the 2000s, the focus of research turned to the personal experiences and the sustainable influence GastarbeiterInnen had on the society, economy, and the urban image of Vienna. At the library of the *Arbeiterkammer* in Vienna, I found data which reflected these changed priorities in the field of immigration studies. Even with this shift, recent ethnological or anthropological works did not examine the obvious connection between the Yugoslavian immigration and its influence on food habits in Austria.

On the one hand, it seems grill specialties like Ćevapčići/ Ćevapi (grilled, minced meat sticks) or Pjeskavica (ground beef or pork patty), are no threat to the Viennese Würstelstand. On the other hand, some people identify the rise of foreign street food vendors with the struggle for existence of the Würstelstand. Is this the manifestation of a cultural frontier in the landscape of street food as Rachel Kay points out in this volume? Are Yugoslavian street food dishes even foreign or part of the culinary heritage of the Habsburg Empire? In fact, former Yugoslavian dishes are seen as a supplement to Austrian street food. Those specialties are seen as typical East-European dishes and are not assigned to a specific state of the former Socialist Federal Republic of Yugoslavia. As such, they are culturally associated with the Würstelstand or the Balkan-Grill. Street food from Bosnia, Croatia, Macedonia, Montenegro, Serbia, and Slovenia theoretically exists but is generally seen as a hybrid or fusion product of different types of Balkan-style Food.

GastarbeiterInnen in a Booming Economy

Until 1962, mainly less-skilled workers from underdeveloped South-East-European countries were labeled as *FremdarbeiterInnen* (foreign workers). *GastarbeiterInnen* replaced the term *FremdarbeiterInnen* because the latter was similar to a term applied to foreign forced labor during the Nazi regime in Austria, and so the connotation was negative. Thus, the term *GastarbeiterInnen* (guest workers) was introduced. It is problematic, because it suggests that the stay of the labor force is temporary and that the recruited people are primarily lured to Austria for economic benefit, rather than being seen as equal partners or guests. While in West Germany in the late 1960s the word was replaced slowly by the term *ausländischer Arbeitnehmer* (foreign jobholder), *GastarbeiterInnen* was still a widespread label in Austria, especially in the mass media.[2]

The GastarbeiterInnen politics in Austria were based on a rotation principle. As a reaction to the lack of manpower, the Austrian government contracted recruitment acts with Spain in 1962, Turkey in 1964, and Yugoslavia in 1966. This meant that the recruitment of workers was internationalized; people were hired in their country of origin to work in Austria within the scope of recruitment for selected industry branches. Already in the 1960s, however, the perspective of permanent employment and settlement with the workers' families replaced this ideal. This

---

2. Leitner, *Gastarbeiter in der städtischen Gesellschaft*, 17.

includes employment tied to the short-term stay of workers mainly from South-East Europe. The Austrian recruitment of foreign workers started later than in West Germany or Switzerland with the actual recruitment taking off in the mid-1960s.[3] By the beginning of the 1970s, the number of foreign workers mounted up steadily and reached its peak with more than 230,000 GastarbeiterInnen in 1973. This massive influx included 178,134 citizens of the Socialist Federal Republic of Yugoslavia.[4]

During this period of the GastarbeiterInnen program, Yugoslavians clearly represented the majority of immigrants. Vienna occupies a special position within Austria due to its large number of GastarbeiterInnen from the Republic of Serbia. In 1974 and 1981, Serbs comprised over 50 percent of the Yugoslavian population of Vienna.[5]

The GastarbeiterInnen-immigration to Vienna can be divided into three periods: The early phase started in the 1960s with the opening of the Austrian job market for immigrants. This period can be seen as the humble beginnings of the Yugoslavian immigration movement. The main phase began in 1970 and lasted until the economic recession of 1973. In the mid-1980s more than the half of all Yugoslavians living in Vienna had originally immigrated during this main phase. The late phase started around 1974. In comparison to German cities, the effects of the economic crisis were not that drastic in Vienna. Even with the ban of recruitment and other restrictions on the job market, an enormous number of Yugoslavian immigrants moved to Vienna. At the beginning of the late phase, a rotation wave under the GastarbeiterInnen was visible. In the mid-1970s, the statistic

---

3. Heinz Faßmann and Rainer Münz, *Einwanderungsland Österreich?: Historische Muster, aktuelle Trends und politische Maßnahmen* (Vienna: Jugend und Volk, 1995), 41.

4. Faßmann and Münz, *Einwanderungsland Österreich?*, 41–47.

5. Elisabeth Lichtenberger, *Gastarbeiter: Leben in zwei Gesellschaften* (Cologne: Böhlau, 1984), 89.

dominance of the Serbian immigrants was weakened through the increasing number of Croatian and Turkish GastarbeiterInnen.[6]

After the setbacks of 1973, the ban of recruitment in 1974 was enacted. This resulted in the end of the international recruitment and the massive cutbacks of the foreign worker quota. By today's standards, the treatment of human beings like a maneuverable mass on the employment market without consideration of their social needs and rights is considered insensitive and disrespectful. Comparing the GastarbeiterInnen in the politics of the 1960s to the *FremdarbeiterInnen* politics during the Nazi-regime, as Heinz Faßmann and Rainer Münz did, might be too polemical, but in fact in both cases the need of national industrial production determined the migration process. The workers were selected, forwarded to Austria, instructed, and housed at the place of destination.[7]

Austria was only one of many North-West-European nations that benefited from the targeted working migration. These immigration-regimes worked with active recruitment, like in Austria, or as a Laissez-faire-regime, like in France.[8] The style of the migration system was also co-determined from the specific history of immigration in the different countries.

The Balkan-Grill: Between Imperial Viennese Tradition and a Balkanized Image of Eastern-Europe

The GastarbeiterInnen movement affected Austrian society sustainably, including the development of food habits in cities.[9]

---

6. Lichtenberger, *Gastarbeiter,* 101.

7. Faßmann and Münz. *Einwanderungsland Österreich?*, 44.

8. Marcel Berlinghoff, *Das Ende der Gastarbeit: Europäischer Anwerbestopps 1970–1974* (Paderborn: Ferdinand Schöningh, 2013), 13–23.

9. Erol Yildiz, "Was heißt hier 'Parallelgesellschaft?': Vom öffentlichen Diskurs zur Lebenspraxis," in *50 Jahre türkische Gastarbeit in Österreich: Wissenschaftliche Analysen/ Lebensgeschichten*, ed. Ali Özbaş, Joachim Heinzl, and Handan Özbaş (Graz: Leykam, 2014), 61–64.

Although many immigrants became Austrian citizens and their children were born and raised in Austria, they were still confronted with racial stereotypes and were alleged of creating a parallel society. Viennese people often forget that the city itself and many aspects of urban life that seem to be traditionally Viennese, were products of the bridge function of the city and its multi-ethnic history, which dates back to the Habsburg Empire. In daily life these references are indeed clearly assigned in language, family names, street names, conventional practices and, of course, in Viennese cuisine.[10]

In this case, the link between Yugoslavian or Balkan-style dishes and Viennese Cuisine is obvious. Specialties like Ćevapčići/Ćevapi or Pjeskavica were popular dishes in Vienna at least since the eighteenth century.[11] Even the term Ćevapčići exemplifies the transformation of the naming of dishes through immigration. While the name Ćevapi is common in former Yugoslavian countries, in Austria and other German-speaking destinations of the GastarbeiterInnen movements the term changed via the old-fashioned word "Ćići" of the eighteenth century to the combined terminus Ćevapčići, which is popular in Austria today.[12] For this reason Serbian and Croatian dishes, as well as Bohemian or Hungarian dishes, were often seen as a part of the legacy of the multi-ethnic monarchy, and because of this, barely recognized as foreign, independent cuisines. This fusion of various national cuisines and the description of the Viennese cuisine as an archive of national identity constructions are mirrored by the naming of dishes with national identifiers. Serbian Bean Soup, Bosnian Gulasch or the Krainer-Sausage (*Kranjska Klobasa*; *Krain* was the former name of

---

10. Peter Eppel, "Einleitung," in *Wir: zur Geschichte und Gegenwart der Zuwanderung nach Wien*, Sonderausstellung des Historischen Museums der Stadt Wien 217, ed. Peter Eppel, (Vienna: Eigenverlag der Wiener Museen, 1996), 6.

11. Wolfgang Rohrbach, "Auf den Spuren der Serben Wiens," *Wiener Geschichtsblätter* 56, no.3 (2001): 186.

12. Rohrbach. "Auf den Spuren der Serben Wiens," 186.

a part of the Habsburg Empire populated mainly by Slovenians, which were colloquially called *Kranjec*) are just a few examples.[13]

Although there was comprehensive Yugoslavian influence, Serbian, Croatian and Bosnian dishes were also an integral part of Viennese cuisine and were offered in restaurants that focused on Austrian or Hungarian specialties. After the end of World War I and the fall of the Habsburg Empire, the close relationship between those cooking styles remained constant. Culinary-wise, the Habsburg Empire of the nineteenth century developed a surprising cohesiveness.[14] The rising trend is to push the label of "authentic" Viennese cuisine which really draws upon this imperial legacy. The consequence of this marketing strategy is that Viennese dishes are presented as an amalgamative, specialized form of cuisine sold in the city center, whereas dishes that are sold outside of imperial Vienna are labeled as *Hausmannskost* (Austrian plain fare).[15]

The fusion of Viennese cuisine managed to include various East-European influences without significant difficulty. The ambiguity of the gastro-cultural borders was closely related to the nation-building process and the consequential invention of national cuisines; however even nationalized dishes were often superimposed by the state.[16]

In contrast to this picture of a well-known, allied food culture of Yugoslavia in Vienna, is the image of competition with

---

13. Julia Danielczyk and Birgit Peter, "Die Transnationale des Geschmacks: Wiener Küche als 'Archiv' von Identitätskonstruktionen," in *Kulinarik und Kultur: Speisen als kulturelle Codes in Zentraleuropa*, ed. Moritz Csáky and Georg-Christian Lack, 68–82. (Vienna: Böhlau, 2014).

14. Bernhardt Tschofen, "Nahrungsforschung und Multikultur: Eine Wiener Skizze," Österreichische Zeitschrift für Volkskunde 96 (1993): 125–45.

15. Konrad Köstlin, "Die Wiener Küche: Ein Alleinstellungsmerkmal avant la letter," in *Kulinarik und Kultur: Speisen als kulturelle Codes in Zentraleuropa*, ed. Moritz Csáky and Georg-Christian Lack (Vienna: Böhlau, 2014), 121–31.

16. Maren Möhring, *Fremdes Essen: Die Geschichte der ausländischen Gastronomie in der Bundesrepublik Deutschland* (Munich: Oldenbourg, 2012), 325.

cuisine associated with cultures of the former Ottoman Empire. It becomes obvious that the close relationship between Balkan and Ottoman cooking traditions can be understood through the style of preparation and the names of similar dishes. The Serbo-Croat term Ćevapčići/Ćevapi is related to the Turkish or Persian expression "*Kebap*."[17] The Bosnian "*Burek*" sounds virtually the same as the Turkish word "*Börek*". The preparation of these dishes is nearly identical. Other overlapping specialties are grilled mutton dishes and stuffed vegetables.[18]

Maybe it was the combination of perceptions of Yugoslavian cuisine as both a familiar part of the Viennese cuisine and as an exotic, unknown (and partially Orientalized) Ottoman cuisine that attracted the Austrian consumers after World War II. Maren Möhring points out that, in this regard, the so-called Balkanism, despite many Orientalized elements, is not just another form of Orientalism. She argues that Balkanism assumes differences inside of one type, whereas Orientalism supposes differences between different types.[19]

The Balkan was not seen as the completely foreign other, but was instead a less familiar and distant relative in a West-European discourse. So the Balkan was marginalized, but still part of the European culture and not the prime target of othering.[20] Due to the rising number of GastarbeiterInnen, the terms "Yugoslavia" and "Balkan" were ever-present. This probably influenced the wild imagination of Yugoslavian food unconsciously as well, because of the widespread stereotypes in the Austrian mass media. It is ascertainable from the coverage of the 1970s-media that there were many analogies made in the coverage of mentally

17. Hedda Reindl-Kiel, "Wesirfinger und Frauenschenkel: Zur Sozialgeschichte der türkischen Küche", *Archiv für Kulturgeschichte* 77, no.1 (1995): 60.
18. Möhring. *Fremdes Essen*, 325.
19. Möhring. *Fremdes Essen*, 328–29.
20. Maria Todorova, *Imagining the Balkans* (Oxford: Oxford University Press, 1997), 38.

ill GastarbeiterInnen.[21] Additionally Yugoslavians had to face widespread, racist abuses in public like *Tschusch* or *Kanake*, which were pejorative terms for immigrants from South-East-Europe in Austria. After 1989, the increasing influx of Yugoslavian and citizens of the former Soviet Union triggered a controversial debate about immigration policies, polarizing the Austrian public.[22]

To attempt to identify a particular Yugoslavian national identity is problematic, because even in former Yugoslavia, the designation "Yugoslavian" was not introduced until the third after-war census in 1961. This term was rather uncommon and unpopular among the citizens in comparison to a closer ethnic regional naming such as Serb or Croat. In 1961, less than two percent of the population labeled themselves as Yugoslavian.[23]

The change from Serbian-Croatian cuisine to Balkan-style street food is closely related to the trends of eating habits in Central-Europe and the steadily increasing number of foreign workers in Austria since the 1950s. Before the period of GastarbeiterInnen policies, the street food trend was pushed forward by the eating habits of American soldiers, who were used to eating on the go. The resulting street food culture can be seen as introduced by foreign soldiers after World War II.

Other important factors for the changes in eating culture in Austria were the travelling wave (*Reisewelle*, responsible for the interest in exotic food of many people), the munching wave (*Fresswelle*, a massive increase per capita of plentiful food), the new snack culture, and the "food-to-go" trend at the end of the 1950s and at the beginning of the 1960s. The abolition of the strict seating

---

21. Michael Segal, "Das Bild der Gastarbeiter in der Presse: Eine Inhaltsanalytische Untersuchung von Printmedien in Salzburg und München" (PhD diss., University of Salzburg, 1981), 196.

22. Werner Holz and Rainer Münz, *Wissen und Einstellung zu Migration, ausländischer Bevölkerung und staatlicher Ausländerpolitik in Österreich* (Vienna: Institut für Demographie der Österreichischen Akademie der Wissenschaft, 1994), 5.

23. Pascal Goeke, *Transnationale Migrationen: Post-jugoslawische Biografien in der Weltgesellschaft* (Bielefeld: transcript Verlag, 2007), 185.

order during meals was compounded by the spread of the television in countless households and of the ideological fight against such bourgeois rites especially among the 1968-Generation.[24]

These factors were essential for the rise of the so-called Balkan-Grill in Austria. The term conveys that this type of street food vendor represents a whole region in South-East Europe. In comparison to Balkan restaurants, they only offer selected grill-specialties, without claiming to represent a whole culinary region or a unique East-European flair. The borders of the Balkans and its identification as a geographical construct were always hard to define, and, with the assimilation of an enormous number of Yugoslavian GastarbeiterInnen, the level of the foreignness, especially for the former exotic Balkan style dishes, evidently changed. The Balkan-Grill tendered an opportunity for the GastarbeiterInnen to eat familiar dishes and to use these sites as communication centers. In contrast, the chance to engage in an independent profession from the catering industry was unusual, due to numerous labor restrictions for migrants from Yugoslavia. The possibility to obtain permission to run an independent business was not enacted until 2006 through the *Fremdenrechtspaket*. This is a binding list of laws that deal with rights of foreign nationals in Austria—a number of which sustainably facilitated the access to independent professions for nationals of non-member states of the European Economic Area like Albania, Bosnia-Herzegovina, Macedonia, Montenegro, and Serbia.[25]

It is possible that these restrictive laws of the past lingered in the memory of the Yugoslavian GastarbeiterInnen and their relatives. This could, in any case, be a possible explanation for the conspicuous under-representation of people from former Yugo-

---

24. Gunther Hirschfelder, *Europäische Esskultur: Geschichte der Ernährung von der Steinzeit bis heute* (Frankfurt am Main: Campus, 2001), 243–57.

25. "Arbeitsmigration nach Österreich in der Zweiten Republik," Demokratiezentrum Wien, accessed December 12, 2014, http://www.demokratiezentrum.org/wissen/timelines/arbeitsmigration-nach-oesterreich-in-der-zweiten-republik.html.

slavia (excluding Slovenia) in independent jobs nowadays.[26]

No country—excluding former Yugoslavia and Germany—experienced the spread of Yugoslavian and Balkan-style restaurants and street food dishes between the 1950s and 1970s, as extensively as Austria did. Only the rise of Italian cuisine in Austria and Germany is more prominent than this successful sprawl of foreign food. Besides the historical affinity of Balkanized cuisine in Austria, two major events made this development possible. On the one hand, the GastarbeiterInnen immigration movement clearly influenced the rise of the Balkan Grill. On the other hand, the role of former Yugoslavia as popular holiday destination during this period made a considerable contribution to the vending of Yugoslavian specialties in Vienna.

Another important reason for the success of the Balkan-Grill and Balkan-style snack bars was the double marketing strategy of presenting Yugoslavian snacks as traditionally part of the Viennese cuisine, and at the same time as fulfilling the stereotype of a spicy culinary adventure dominated by the taste of garlic and various peppers. The blending of familiar food habits, the composition of known ingredients, and an exotic touch met the expectations of Austrian customers in the 1960s and 1970s. After the 1980s, however, the Balkan-Grill became unpopular due to the competition of other cheap, semi-exotic snacks like the Döner Kebab. In the 1980s, the reason for the former success of selling products that combined known food with a foreign touch, as well as meat-dominated dishes, did not work any longer. The uniformity of food habits and the Balkan War in the 1990s hastened the decline of the Balkan Grill.[27]

---

26. Nina Birner, "Erwerbstätige Zuwander/innen in Österreich" in *Österreichischer Integrations Fond-Dossier* 33 (Vienna: ÖIF, 2014), 17.

27. Maren Möhring, "Balkan-Grill und Chinarestaurant: Migration und Konsum ausländischer Speisen in der Bundesrepublik Deutschland." In Über den Tellerrand geschaut: Migration und Ernährung in historischer Perspektive (18. bis 20. Jahrhundert.), ed. Mathias Beer, (Essen: Klartextverlag, 2014), 221–42.

Although the changes of the GastarbeiterInnens' eating habits in gastronomy and street food offerings in Vienna were obvious, the impacts last even longer. At the beginning of the 1990s, restaurant and snack bars that offered so-called former Yugoslavian and Turkish GastarbeiterInnen cuisine (alongside Italian and Greek cuisine) dominated the foreign gastronomy scene in Vienna.[28]

Furthermore, it is important to explore how GastarbeiterInnen influenced the market culture of Vienna. After a brief off-topic research, it seems that many of the markets in the city that are nowadays hotspots of tourism and social life were nearly removed from the cityscape in the 1980s, because of their lack of attractiveness. Recent literature highlights the essential role of the GastarbeiterInnen during the process of revitalizing these places and making them attractive for potential customers. Current popular market places such as the *Naschmarkt* and the *Brunnenmarkt* in Vienna represent this success story. They owe their image as culinary hotspots, central terminals of information and communication, and as alternative places in an urbanized, anonymous city to the immigrants that created a picturesquely marketable image.[29]

Rediscovered Traces of the GastarbeiterInnen
—A Conclusion

Migration movements have had an impact on the street food culture of Vienna in the twentieth century. The GastarbeiterInnen migration was not the only influence on street food in Vienna, but Turkish immigrants also brought new tastes to the city. Yugoslavian GastarbeiterInnen as consumers and vendors of street food helped to create an identity of their cuisine that

---

28. Tuschofen," Nahrungsforschung und Multikultur."
29. Sylvia Mattl, "1995: Migration und Gastronomie: Lokalzeile am Naschmarkt, Wien," in *Gastarbajteri: 40 Jahre Arbeitsmigration*, ed. Hakan Gürses, et al. (Vienna: Mandelbaum, 2004), 146–48.

fluctuated between traditional Viennese and fiery Balkan-Style food-culture. Through this double marketing strategy, they succeeded in meeting the taste of the Austrian post-war society.

Yugoslavian snack bars and the Balkan-Grill often combined Austrian and mixed Balkan-style dishes to satisfy the demand of a hybrid of exotic and well-known food. This harmonization was ultimately the reason why, in the 1980s, this type of gastronomy lost its exotic attraction. Generally, the Gastarbeiter-Innen had a lasting impact on the development of street food in Vienna. The transformation of dishes from the Viennese cuisine into snacks-to-go offers distinct examples of this process. Also the hybrids of the Viennese Würstelstand and the Balkan-Grill culture, like the Bosna-Hot-Dog or the inclusion of Ćevapčići in the Würstelstand repertoire testify to this.

Although the Yugoslavian GastarbeiterInnen community of Vienna in the 1970s lived rather frugally, and dining in local restaurants or cafes was unusual, visiting a street food vendor or a Balkan-Grill in contrast was quite popular, because of the reasonable prices and the function of such places as meeting points.[30]

The fast and familiar food of the Balkan-Grill met two major needs of the immigrants, the requirement of mobile, flexible, and cheap food, especially during the lunch break; and the want for a symbolic piece of home. Food is still considered one of the strongest means to create and preserve the cultural identity of immigrants, and it has preserved a microcosm of Habsburg variety in the city of Vienna.[31]

---

30. Institut für empirische Sozialforschung Wien (IFES), Gastarbeiter in Wien: I. Jugoslawen. (Vienna: IFES, 1973), 10.
31. Roman Sandgruber, "Österreichische Nationalspeisen: Mythos und Realität," in *Essen und kulturelle Identität: Europäische Perspektiven*, ed. Hans Jürgen Teuteberg et al. (Berlin: Akademie Verlag, 1997).

Bibliography

Amenda, Lars, and Ernst Langthaler, eds. *Kulinarische "Heimat" und "Fremde": Migration und Ernährung im 19. und 20. Jahrhundert.* Jahrbuch für Geschichte des ländlichen Raumes 10 Innsbruck: Studienverlag, 2014.

Bauer, Werner. *Zuwanderung nach Österreich.* Vienna: Österreichische Gesellschaft für Politikberatung und Politikentwicklung, 2008.

Berlinghoff, Marcel. *Das Ende der Gastarbeit: Europäischer Anwerbestopps 1970–1974.* Paderborn: Ferdinand Schöningh, 2013.

Birner, Nina. "Erwerbstätige Zuwander/innen in Österreich." In *Österreichischer Integrations Fond-Dossier* 33, 1–53. Vienna: ÖIF, 2014.

Csáky, Moritz, and Georg-Christian Lack, eds. *Kulinarik und Kultur: Speisen als kulturelle Codes in Zentraleuropa.* Vienna: Böhlau, 2014

Danielczyk, Julia, and Birgit Peter. "Die Transnationale des Geschmacks: Wiener Küche als 'Archiv' von Identitätskonstruktionen." In *Kulinarik und Kultur: Speisen als kulturelle Codes in Zentraleuropa,* edited by Moritz Csáky and Georg-Christian Lack, 68–82. Vienna: Böhlau, 2014.

Dantine, Wilhelm. *Gastarbeiter: Befragung von Schlüsselpersonen im Freizeitmilieu.* Vienna: Arbeitskreis für ökonomische und soziologische Studien, 1972.

Eppel, Peter. "Einleitung." In *Wir: zur Geschichte und Gegenwart der Zuwanderung nach Wien.* Sonderausstellung des Historischen Museums der Stadt Wien 217, edited by Peter Eppel. Wien: Eigenverlag der Wiener Museen, 1996.

Faßmann, Heinz, and Rainer Münz. *Einwanderungsland Österreich? Historische Muster, aktuelle Trends und politische Maßnahmen.* Vienna: Jugend und Volk, 1995.

Fischer, Wladimir. "Migrant Voices in the Contemporary History of Vienna. The Case of Ex-Yugoslavs." In *Constructing Urban Memories: The Role of Oral Testimony,* edited by Cynthia Brown and Richard Rodger, 231–49. Aldershot: Ashgate, 2007.

Goeke, Pascal. *Transnationale Migrationen: Post-jugoslawische Biografien in der Weltgesellschaft.* Bielefeld: transcript Verlag, 2007.

Gürses, Hakan, Cornelia Kogoj Cornelia, and Sylvia Mattl. *Gastarbajteri: 40 Jahre Arbeitsmigration.* Vienna: Mandelbaum, 2004.

Haberl, Othmar Nikola. *Die Abwanderung von Arbeitskräften aus Jugoslawien: Zur Problematik ihrer Auslandsbeschäftigung und Rückführung.* München: Oldenbourg, 1978.

Hischfelder, Gunther. "Pelmeni, Pizze, Piroggi: Determinanten kultureller Identität im Kontext europäischer Küchen Systeme." In *Russische Küche und kulturelle Identität,* edited by Norbert Franz, 31–50. Potsdam: Universitätsverlag Potsdam, 2013.

———. *Europäische Esskultur: Geschichte der Ernährung von der Steinzeit bis heute.* Frankfurt am Main: Campus, 2001. 243–57.

Holz, Werner, and Münz, Rainer. *Wissen und Einstellung zu Migration, ausländischer Bevölkerung und staatlicher Ausländerpolitik in Österreich.* Vienna: Institut für Demographie der Österreichischen Akademie der Wissenschaft, 1994.

Institut für empirische Sozialforschung Wien (IFES). *Gastarbeiter in Wien: I. Jugoslawen.* Vienna: IFES, 1973.

Köstlin, Konrad. "Die Wiener Küche: Ein Alleinstellungsmerkmal avant la lettre." In *Kulinarik und Kultur: Speisen als kulturelle Codes in Zentraleuropa,* edited by Moritz Csáky and Georg-Christian Lack, 121–31. Vienna: Böhlau, 2014.

John, Michael, and Albert Lichtblau. "Labor Migration in Vienna in the Era of Franz Josef: Images and Expectations." In *Expectations of Labor Migrants,* edited by Dirk Hoerder, 100–32. New York: Columbia University Press, 1994.

———. *Schmelztiegel Wien - einst und jetzt: Geschichte und Gegenwart von Zuwanderung und Minderheiten.* Cologne: Böhlau, 1990.

Leitner, Helga. *Gastarbeiter in der städtischen Gesellschaft: Segregation, Integration und Assimilation von Arbeitsmigranten; Am Beispiel jugoslawischer Gastarbeiter in Wien.* Frankfurt am Main: Campus, 1983.

Lichtenberger, Elisabeth. *Gastarbeiter: Leben in zwei Gesellschaften.* Cologne: Böhlau, 1984.

Meindl, Thomas. "Wohnverhältnisse der Gastarbeiter in Wien: Stadtentwicklung vor dem Hintergrund eines segmentierten Arbeits- und Wohnungsmarktes." Diploma thesis, Vienna University of Technology, 1994.

Möhring, Maren. "Balkan-Grill und Chinarestaurant: Migration und Konsum ausländischer Speisen in der Bundesrepublik Deutschland." In *Über den Tellerrand geschaut: Migration und Ernährung in historischer Perspektive* (*18. bis 20. Jahrhundert*), edited by Mathias Beer, 221–42. Essen: Klartext, 2014.

———. *Fremdes Essen: Die Geschichte der ausländischen Gastronomie in der Bundesrepublik Deutschland.* Munich: Oldenbourg, 2012.

Musner, Lutz. *Der Geschmack von Wien: Kultur und Habitus einer Stadt.* Frankfurt am Main: Campus, 2009.

Oltmer, Jochen, Axel Kreienbrink, and Carlos Sanz Díaz, eds. *Das "Gastarbeiter"- System: Arbeitsmigration und ihre Folgen in der Bundesrepublik Deutschland und Westeuropa.* Munich: Oldenbourg, 2012.

Pohl, Hans Dieter. *Die österreichische Küchensprache: Ein Lexikon der typisch österreichischen kulinarischen Besonderheiten mit sprachwissenschaftlichen Erläuterungen.* Vienna: Praesens, 2007.

Reindl-Kiel, Hedda. "Wesirfinger und Frauenschenkel: Zur Sozialgeschichte der türkischen Küche." *Archiv für Kulturgeschichte* 77, no. 1 (1995).

Rohrbach, Wolfgang. "Auf den Spuren der Serben Wiens." *Wiener Geschichtsblätter* 56, no. 3 (2001).

Sandgruber, Roman. "Österreichische Nationalspeisen: Mythos und Realität." In *Essen und kulturelle Identität: Europäische Perspektiven,* edited by Hans Jürgen Teuteberg, Gerhard Neumann, and Alois Wierlacher, 179–203. Berlin: Akademie Verlag, 1997.

Schmidlechner, Karin. "Migrationstheorien und historischer Rückblick mit besonderer Berücksichtigung der Arbeitsmigration in der Steiermark." In *Migration und Arbeit in der Steiermark,* edited by Karin Schmidlechner, Anette Sprung, and Ute Sonnleitner. Graz: Leykam, 2013.

Segal, Michael. "Das Bild der Gastarbeiter in der Presse: Eine Inhaltsanalytische Untersuchung von Printmedien in Salzburg und München." PhD diss., University of Salzburg, 1981.

Šunjic, Melita, and Patrick-Paul Volf, eds. *Echte Österreicher: Gespräche mit Menschen, die als Flüchtlinge ins Land gekommen sind.* Vienna: Picus, 1995.

Todorova, Maria. *Imagining the Balkans.* Oxford: Oxford University Press, 1997.

Tschofen, Bernhardt. "Nahrungsforschung und Multikultur: Eine Wiener Skizze." *Österreichische Zeitschrift für Volkskunde* 96 (1993): 125–45.

Volf, Patrik-Paul. "Der politische Flüchtling als Symbol der Zweiten Republik: Zur Asyl- und Flüchtlingspolitik seit 1945." *Zeitgeschichte* 11–12 (1995): 415–35.

Weilguni, Werner. Österreichisch-Jugoslawische Kulturbeziehungen 1945-1989. Munich: Oldenbourg, 1990.

Yildiz, Erol. "Was heißt hier 'Parallelgesellschaft?' Vom öffentlichen Diskurs zur Lebenspraxis." In *50 Jahre türkische Gastarbeit in Österreich: Wissenschaftliche Analysen/ Lebensgeschichten*, edited by Ali Özbaş, Joachim Heinzl, and Handan Özbag. Graz: Leykam, 2014.

Kurdish Mussels on the Bosporus: How Immigration, Street Food, and Urban Planning Meet in Istanbul

Nicolas Horky

The aim of this article is to examine the topics of migration and street food in Istanbul and how these two themes are related and connected to each other. I have chosen Istanbul as my area of investigation because of the city's unique location spanning two continents, and the ubiquitous street food offerings I observed there during a personal trip in 2014. The outcome is a portrait of the dynamic city of Istanbul through these lenses. My data is based on literature and film documentaries related to these topics, but I also relied on newspaper articles for reasons of availability.

Istanbul has a multiethnic and multicultural history spanning centuries and is famous for its variegated street food supply, which is glorified by travel reports, blogs, and travel guides.[1] There are even commercial tourist agencies offering street food tours.[2] The culture of street food has a longer tradition in the south of Turkey because of climactic conditions; however, it came to the urban center of Istanbul through immigration. The food one can buy in Istanbul's streets is a mix of different regional foods.[3]

---

1. Manfred Ferner, *Istanbul und Umgebung: City Guide* (Bielefeld: Reise Know How Verlag Peter Rump, 2012), 59; Simarprit, "Istanbul Street Food Tour – Istanbul eats on its streets," Allwonders Travel Blog, last modified August 25, 2015, http://www.allwonders.com/blog/tours/istanbul-street-food; and Renate Steigemann, Bernhard Weisser, and Hans E. Latzk, *Istanbul.* (Munich: Polyglott Verlag, 2001), 26.

2. Viator, "Istanbul: Tour mit Straßenessen und Picknick," accessed January 7, 2015, http://www.viatorcom.de/de/7132/tours/Istanbul/Istanbul-Tour-mit-Strassenessen-und-Picknick/d585-5966PICNIC.

3. Katrin Wißmann, "The Taste of a City," *Food Service Europe & Middle East* 1 (2010): 37.

The city of Istanbul is also well known for its immense population growth rate driven by immigration. Due to its geographical location, Istanbul has been a hotspot for trade and commerce for millennia. The movement of goods also involved the flow of people through and to the city. It was the capital of the Byzantine Empire (395–1453) as well as of the Ottoman Empire, which existed until 1923.[4] Although the development of the new political capital in Ankara was central in the early years of the Republic of Turkey, Istanbul remained the economic and cultural capital.[5]

The population of Istanbul has grown rapidly since the end of the Ottoman Empire, from one million inhabitants in 1950 to five million in 1980, and doubling by 2000.[6] Official sources currently count more than fourteen million people living in this city on the Bosporus Strait.[7] This growth is the result of mostly internal migration. In the last fifty years, eleven million Turkish people from eighty-two different regions moved to Istanbul. Most of them were members of financially poor areas who entered the city with their families in search of employment.[8]

In the 1980s, the national economy of Turkey was opened to global markets. Disorganized capitalism, post-Fordism, flexible accumulation, and globalization transformed the social and spatial appearance of Istanbul. Foreign direct investments increased 320-fold between 1980 and 1998. In 2003, more than three-fourths of all

---

4. Neyran Turan, "Towards an Ecological Urbanism for Istanbul," in *Megacities. Urban Form, Governance and Sustainability*, ed. André Sorensen and Junichiro Okata (Tokyo: Springer, 2011), 227.

5. Turan, "Towards an Ecological Urbanism for Istanbul," 229.

6. Caglar Keyder, "Globalization and Social Exclusion in Istanbul," *International Journal of Urban and Regional Research* 29, no. 1 (2005): 125.

7. Türkiye Istatistik Kurumu (Institute of Statistics in Turkey), accessed January 7, 2015, http://tuikapp.tuik.gov.tr/adnksdagitapp/adnks.zul?dil=2.

8. Aysun Çelik, "Binnenmigrationsbewegungen in der Türkei: Konstruierte regionale Beziehungen in der Migration," (diploma thesis, University of Vienna, 2009), 8.

foreign direct investments in Turkey landed in Istanbul.[9] The service sector grew quickly, and manufacturing industries moved out of the city.[10] The status as a center for global capital, as well as the growing population makes Istanbul a classical example for the widespread concept of a global city.[11]

Here I will concentrate on the Kurdish immigration from south-eastern Anatolia to Istanbul which started in the 1960s.[12] The main Kurdish migration occurred during the conflict from the 1990s onwards between the *Partiya Karkerên Kurdistani* (Kurdistan Workers' Party, or PKK) and the Turkish military, which in many cases resulted in relocation.[13] This is the period I focus on in my research.

Many Kurds work in the tourist industry and as street vendors and are linked to the selling of *midye dolma* (stuffed mussels), which can be found in the whole city but especially in areas with considerable pedestrian traffic such as in the neighborhood of Karaköy next to the Galata bridge.[14] I analyze the area of Tarlabaşı, where most of these vendors live. It is located in the district Beyoğlu which has become associated with gentrification and is completely under construction.

In addition to migration, globalization has changed the street food scene in recent decades. On the one hand, new products like

---

9. Turan, "Towards an Ecological Urbanism for Istanbul," 233.

10. Murat Cemal Yalcintan and Adem Erdem Erbas, "Impacts of 'Gecekondu' on the Electoral Geography of Istanbul," *International Labor and Working-Class History* 64 (Fall, 2003): 93.

11. Saskia Sassen, "The Global City: Introducing a Concept," *Brown Journal of World Affairs* 11, no. 2 (2005): 39.

12. Femke Sonnenschein and Toon van Meijl, "Migration and the Dialogue of Multiple Identifications: Kurdish migrants in the tourist industry of Istanbul," *Identities: Global Studies in Culture and Power* 25, no. 5 (2014): 482.

13. Çelik, Binnenmigrationsbewegungen in der Türkei, 36; Maggie Schmitt, "Mussels on the Streets of Istanbul," *The Atlantic*, December 2, 2009, http://www.theatlantic.com/health/archive/2009/12/mussels-on-the-streets-of-istanbul/31058/.

14. Wißmann, "The Taste of a City," 37.

exotic fruits appeared on the streets of Istanbul. On the other hand, vendors now have to deal with new regulations because of the introduction of EU-norms. For example, *simit*, a street food since the Ottoman Empire, has to be sold behind glass windows instead of open carts to abide by the law. Authorized street food sellers, however, are the exception; most of the vendors operate illegally.[15] Vendors are vulnerable to prosecution but are often unable to follow government regulations, as I explain in the case of midye dolma. In general, the number of street vendors is presently decreasing.[16]

Midye Dolma and Kurdish Vendors

Midye dolma are one of the most famous ready-to-eat foods in the streets of Istanbul. They are mussels and rice, which are cooked separately and then stuffed together into the shell of the mussel. Other ingredients are black pepper, oil, cinnamon, and other spices. Usually the vendors squeeze fresh lemon juice over the mussel right before eating. In the streets, they are sold individually as finger food for immediate consumption.[17] The mussels are not only present in the waters of the Bosporus. They are common in the whole south-eastern Mediterranean coast. Even in the Turkish capital Ankara, which is far from any sea, stuffed mussels can be bought in the streets.[18] Midye dolma are usually

15. Konuk Mehves and Yavuz Serpil, "Istanbul's Street-food Vendors, Municipal Officers Disagree on Regulations," *Hürriyet Daily News*, August 4, 2010, http://www.hurriyetdailynews.com/default.aspx?pageid=438&n=streetside-vendors-and-municipality-officers-disagree-on-street-food-standards-2010-08-04.
16. Wißmann, "The Taste of a City," 37; and Mehran Kamrava, "The Semi-formal Sector and the Turkish Political Economy," *British Journal of Middle Eastern Studies* 31, no. 1 (2004): 68.
17. Enver Baris Bingol, Hilal Colek, Hamparsun Hampikyan, and Karlo Muratoglu, "The Microbiological Quality of Stuffed Mussels (Midye Dolma) Sold in Istanbul," *British Food Journal* 110, no. 11 (2008), 1080.
18. Mustafa Ates, Asli Ozkizilcik, and Cengiz Tabakoglu, "Microbiological Analysis of Stuffed Mussels Sold in the Streets," *Indian Journal of Microbiology* 51, no. 3 (2011), 350.

served as an appetizer.[19] It is possible to get midye dolma in most crowded places in the city but they are particularly popular near the tourist centers next to the Galata Bridge and near the nightlife street İstiklal Caddesi. It is common for Turks, as well as for foreigners, to consume the mussels while on the go.

For street food vendors, it is often a cat-and-mouse game with municipal patrol officers. To sell food legally, they need an *İşgaliye*, a street food sale authorization. In general, the authorization is difficult to obtain and many vendors cannot afford the monthly fee, differing according to every district in town. To be licensed, the municipality inspects the type of food, the cart and the dressing of the vendors. In the case of midye dolma, the situation is even more complicated. Simply, no license is available. Therefore, all street vendors of midye dolma are acting without any permission.[20] On the other hand, official sources from 2004 point out that the vendors were controlled by the city's Chamber of Commerce, regarding the quality of their product because some consumers had become fatally ill.[21] A microbiological study about health risks of eating mussels in the streets of Istanbul showed that they can contain E. Coli, salmonella, and heavy metals; and excess consumption is not recommended.[22] A similar and more recent study of midye dolma sold in Ankara showed that more than 75 percent of the chosen sample of 600 stuffed mussels were simply unacceptable according to the criteria of the Turkish *Codex Alimentarius* which lays out the regulatory framework of quality control in the preparation and serving of food.[23]

---

19. Clifford Endres, "Edouard Roditi and the Istanbul Avant-Garde," *Texas Studies in Literature and Language* 54, no. 4 (2012): 12.
20. Mehveş and Serpil, "Istanbul's Street-food Vendors."
21. Kamrava, "The Semi-formal Sector", 68.
22. Bingol, Colek, Hampikyan, and Muratoglu, "The Microbiological Quality of Stuffed Mussels," 1085.
23. Ates, Ozkizilcik, and Tabakoglu, "Microbiological Analysis of Stuffed Mussels," 353.

However, there also exist voices stating that the defamation of stuffed mussels clearly is linked to the immigration background of the vendors due to chain migration and business networks.[24] Selling mussels was the only possibility for Kurdish newcomers to the city to escape from jobless poverty.[25] The Kurds, coming mostly from highlands far away from the sea, did not bring the knowledge of mussel preparation to Istanbul. It was commonly known that before Kurds sold mussels in Istanbul, Armenians did. Through friendship between Armenians and Kurds, this business was overtaken by Kurds sometime in the 1990s.[26]

The Turkish/Kurdish filmmaker Güliz Sağlam created a documentary about people from the area of Mardin in south-east Anatolia near the border of Syria and Iraq called *Li Durî Malê/ Evden Uzakta/Far Away From Home*. Most of the subjects were living in Tarlabaşı and earned their money in the mussel business. An anonymous woman in the film states that "in this area everybody is earning their living by mussels."[27] One protagonist of the documentary tells about the struggles with the police, stating that they often hit him because of his Kurdish roots. He quotes that the general perception police officers have of Kurdish people in Istanbul is that they are all terrorists.[28] Similar statements are often mentioned by Kurds in Istanbul.[29]

---

24. Iris Anliamater, "Illegal Food Systems: Street Mussels in Istanbul," TheMiracalOfFeedingCities.com (blog), July 18, 2014, http://miracleofeedingcities.com/illegal-food-systems-street-mussels-in-istanbul/.

25. Schmitt, "Mussels on the Streets of Istanbul."

26. Güliz Sağlam. *Li Durî Malê / Evden Uzakta / Far Away From Home*, 2003, DVD, 29 min, 26:50.

27. Sağlam. *Li Durî Malê*, 17:00.

28. Sağlam. *Li Durî Malê*, 3:24.

29. Murat Ergin, "The Racialization of Kurdish Identity in Turkey," *Ethnic and Racial Studies* 37 No 2 (2014), 322; and Anna Secor, "'There Is an Istanbul That Belongs to Me': Citizenship, Space, and Identity in the City," *Annals of the Association of American Geographers* 94, no. 2 (2004), 352, 359.

Sağlam's film shows how some of the vendors harvest the mussels directly from the Bosporus. Some of the collectors learned swimming and especially diving in Istanbul. Others say that there are at least three kinds of mussel traders coming every day, ranging from individuals to larger, commercial operations.[30] Because of the unclear working conditions in the business, it is hard to find out how it is organized. During my private trip in 2014, I observed people diving and collecting mussels at the peer of Üsküdar, on the Asian side of the city; it was unclear, however, if their activity was related to economic interests. Beside large local companies, which are selling mussels to restaurants or corner stores, there are websites, such as that of the Midye Dünyası company, where mussels can be ordered online.[31] The company operates from Manisa, more than 500 kilometers away from Istanbul. There are also vendors in the midye dolma business selling products imported from far beyond the waters of the Bosporus.

The gathering, preparing, and selling of street food all include delineated gender roles. Hande Bozdogan from the Istanbul Culinary Institute mentions how "women prepare the foodstuff at home which their husbands or sons then sell on the streets."[32] In *Far Away From Home,* an anonymous young woman, who has been preparing mussels nearly her whole life, tells how she has lived in Istanbul for twelve years and has not yet seen the seaside. She spends every day preparing mussels and managing the household.[33]

Güliz Sağlam, who has been observing the midye dolma-scene for years, emailed me that the vendors are still of Kurdish origin despite being forced to leave their home districts and move to the outskirts of the city, far away from areas of major demand. She also observes that the number of vendors has been decreasing over the years as a result of gentrification, displacement, and governmental regulations.

---

30. Sağlam. *Li Durî Malê,* 17:00.

31. http://www.midyedunyasi.com, accessed January 7, 2015.

32. Hande Bozdogan quoted by Wißmann, "The Taste of a City," 37.

33. Sağlam, *Li Durî Malê,* 13:00.

Migrating to the Bosporus

With the development of 1950s, immigration to Istanbul grew on a large scale. The mechanization and commercialization of agriculture played a major role in this process by displacing workers. Turkish cities and Istanbul, in particular were flooded with people from rural areas searching for work. From 1950 to 1965, the population of Istanbul doubled to more than two million.[34] Istanbul can be seen as a classical example of the global urbanization process which took place in the second half of the twentieth century. In the 1920s, the population of Istanbul was only 4 percent of the total inhabitants of Turkey. Today, different sources place that number between 17 and 20 percent.[35] In the 1960s, the city stretched thirty kilometers on the European and Asian continents; today the urban sprawl stretches eighty kilometers to the west and forty to the east.[36]

This resulted in an enormous housing shortage in Istanbul. Informal forms of housing were enacted faster than every governmental program. Today, more than half of the population of Istanbul is still living in areas called *Gecekondu* (illegal or built-overnight cities), which became the dominant form of urbanization.[37]

Seventy-five percent of the population lives in such areas. The houses were constructed by immigrants at the borders of the cities, near the industrial centers, and also in inner-city districts. The idea of informal housing was derived from the Ottoman legal system where all land was public and belonged to the state. In inner-city districts, Gecekondu settlement consists mainly of squat-

---

34. Turan, "Towards an Ecological Urbanism for Istanbul," 230–31.

35. Turan, "Towards an Ecological Urbanism for Istanbul," 223.

36. Zeynep Merey Enlil, "The Neoliberal Agenda and the Changing Urban Form of Istanbul," *International Planning Studies* 16, no. 1 (2011): 11.

37. Bruce Stanley, "Istanbul," in *Cities of the Middle East and North Africa: A Historical Encyclopedia*, ed. Michael Dumper and Bruce Stanley (Santa Barbara: ABC-Clio, 2007), 187.

ting, sometimes followed by a degree of ownership later. In Gecekondu areas, economic activities are usually as informal as the housing itself. The characteristics of the inhabitants are young, uneducated, und unemployed.[38] The first examples of Gecekondu trace back to the 1940s.[39] After the 1980s, informal housing grew enormously with the possibility to make money through commercialization. This policy became famous under the term *yap-tap* (build and sell). It is nearly impossible to separate these commercially driven, informal housing projects from the Gecekondu construction for reasons of survival.[40] The de-industrialization of the city, starting in the 1980s, affected migrants who were often unskilled and could not easily transition into other opportunities in the service sector, which led to increased participation in informal economic activities.[41]

Most of the immigration to Istanbul in the twentieth century can be described as chain migration, which is "movement in which prospective migrants learn of opportunities, are provided with transportation, and have initial accommodation and employment arranged *by means of primary social relationships with previous migrants.*"[42] Immigration was shaped by a solidarity network, related to families, ethnic groups, or simply place of origin. This migration was mostly voluntary; however, starting in 1984, an additional motive for migration changed Istanbul.

---

38. Keyder, "Globalization and Social Exclusion in Istanbul," 126; and Yalcintan, and Erbas, "Impacts of 'Gecekondu,'" 91, 99.

39. Yalcintan and Erbas, "Impacts of 'Gecekondu,'" 96.

40. Yalcintan and Erbas, "Impacts of 'Gecekondu,'" 94; and Enlil, "The Neoliberal Agenda," 13.

41. Yalcintan, and Erbas, "Impacts of 'Gecekondu,'" 94.

42. John S. MacDonald and Leatrice D. MacDonald, "Chain Migration Ethnic Neighborhood Formation and Social Networks," *The Milbank Memorial Fund Quarterly* 42, no. 1 (1964), 82.

Kurdish Migration, Tarlabaşı & Gentrification

Most Kurdish people live in the south-east of Turkey, Iraq, Iran, and Syria. With about twenty to twenty-five million members, Kurds are one of the most numerous ethnic groups without a state. In the whole of Turkey, 14 to 16 percent of the inhabitants are ethnically Kurds. Since the 1950s, the percentage of Kurds in the cities of Western-Turkey has constantly risen. This first wave of Kurdish immigration lasted until the 1980s and included individuals forced from rural areas through the process of urbanization. The second wave originates from the armed conflict between the PKK and the Turkish military that started in 1984. In the course of this conflict, which dominated Turkish politics in the 1990s, two to three million people were internally displaced. The conflict goes back to the early Republic of Turkey in the 1920s and the policies of nationalism as well as the construction of Turkishness under Mustafa Kemal Atatürk, the founder of the Republic. Languages other than Turkish were forbidden (the three main Kurdish languages are Kurmancî, Soranî, and Zaza), and a Kurdish identity or ethnicity was silenced for the sake of assimilation of the so called future-Turks or mountain-Turks.[43] In the 1990s, more than 1,000 villages in the districts with mainly Kurdish populations were destroyed which left hundreds of thousands of people homeless.[44] Today there exist forty-eight different ethnic communities in Istanbul, with Kurds comprising the major group. Due to the Kurdish immigration from south-east Anatolia, Istanbul can be considered the largest Kurdish city in the world.[45]

These forced newcomers to the Western cities were confronted with exclusion and anti-Kurdish sentiments based on racial and economic reservations. Kurds were often constrained to self-em-

---

43. Ergin, "The Racialization Tof Kurdish Identity," 324–25; and Secor, "'There Is an Istanbul That Belongs to Me,'" 353–56.

44. Keyder, "Globalization and Social Exclusion in Istanbul," 132.

45. Stanley, "Istanbul," 187.

ployment with informal commercial activities or unclear working conditions, for example as street vendors, since Kurdishness carries an association with criminality.[46] Today it is still harder to find a job in Istanbul when somebody declares his or her Kurdish background.[47] Compared to migration before the 1990s, a rise in social and economic position was far more difficult for Kurds because they lacked proper networks for labor or housing markets.[48]

Many of the neighborhoods where the new immigrants in the cities lived, often Gecekondu, were regionally, religiously, and ethnically segregated spaces.[49] One example for a Gecekondu was the district of Tarlabaşı. When I write about Tarlabaşı, I use past tense because today it is completely under construction. With the rising inequality, gentrification, a process observed in various cities around the world, started in certain districts of Istanbul in the 1980s and increased sharply over the last decade. It could be divided in three waves. Tarlabaşı was located in the highly gentrified district of Beyoğlu, near the pedestrian boulevard İstiklal Caddesi. Beyoğlu became the main center for cinemas, theatres, art galleries as well as bars, cafés and all kinds of shopping supply in the second gentrification wave at the end of the last millennium.[50] Tarlabaşı's size is about two hectares. Historically it was the residential area of non-Muslim middle class (mostly Genoese, Greeks, and Armenians) that, in the 1990s, was inhabited by mostly Kurdish refugees.[51] For foreign visitors, this area remained

---

46. Ergin, "The Racialization of Kurdish identity," 329–32.
47. Secor, "'There Is an Istanbul That Belongs to Me,'" 362.
48. Enlil, "The Neoliberal Agenda," 20.
49. Secor, "'There Is an Istanbul That Belongs to Me,'" 362.
50. Enlil, "The Neoliberal Agenda," 21; and Tolga Islam, "Outside the core: Gentrification in Istanbul," in *Gentrification in a Global Context. The new urban colonialism*, ed. Rowland Atkinson and Gary Bridge (London and New York: Routledge, 2005), 133–34.
51. İclal Dinçer, "The Impact of Neoliberal Policies on Historic Urban Space: Areas of Urban Renewal in Istanbul," *International Planning Studies* 16, no. 1 (2011), 43–60.

mostly invisible. Despite being located near one of the tourist hotspots, the local authorities managed to keep these two spaces apart from each other. Tarlabaşı's population was 78 percent immigrants. It was sometimes called a refugee camp, especially for Kurds. In the media, it was presented as a no go area and hotspot of prostitution, crime, and drugs.[52]

In 2006, Tarlabaşı was declared as one of the city's renewal areas. It consisted of nine blocks which equals 278 plots. A private company received the license for demolishing 70 percent of the historical area, and rebuilt it, which entirely changed the resident demography. It was followed by unsuccessful protests and initiatives organized by displaced persons.[53]

The Diversity of Street Food

For the Istanbul-domiciled Nobel Prize in Literature winner in 2006, Orhan Pamuk, consuming street food in Turkey was a way to leave behind Islamic traditions. It started in the twentieth century with the declaration of the Republic of Turkey and the search for modernity. For many people, it was a symbol of progress to consume food that was not homemade by their wives or mothers, or, in other words, food which left the sacred privacy of the household.[54]

In addition to midye dolma described above, the following provides a short overview on some different street foods in Istanbul. These are just famous examples, a complete list of the delicious supply in the megacity is impossible.

---

52. Keyder, "Globalization and Social Exclusion in Istanbul," 128; and David Morley, "Istanbul Tales: David Morley Reflects on the Past and Future of Istanbul," *Soundings* 37 (2007), 51–52.

53. Susanne Maier, *Widerstand & Wäscheleinen: Stadterneuerung und räumliche Taktiken der Gegenkultur eines Vereins und seiner Akteurinnen in Tarlabaşı/Istanbul* (diploma thesis, University of Vienna, 2010), 90–96.

54. Orhan Pamuk, "Forbidden Fare," *The New Yorker,* July 9, 2007, 48.

In general, there are two kinds of street food: prepared food, similar to the meals anyone can order in a restaurant, packed for consuming it on the streets and raw food which is ready for preparation. Most of the food described is exclusive to the streets of Istanbul or Turkey in general. The cuisine offered in restaurants or in the streets is very similar to other southeast Mediterranean cuisines and culinary traditions and are still discussed as expressions of nationalism (for example, between Turks and Armenians or Turks and Greeks).[55] As such, I will not engage in the discussion about the origin of certain products but will instead focus on the foods themselves.

The probably most famous—because it is the most visible—street food is *simit*. Similar to a bagel or a pretzel, it is a round pastry sold in bakeries or classically from carts in the streets. Most simits come with sesame seeds and a buttery glaze, and some are sweeter than others. Its origins date back to Ottoman times about 500 years ago, and it is still very common everywhere in Turkey, the Middle East, and the Balkans. Similar to the case of midye dolma, the simit business nowadays is also linked to migration. In the 1960s immigrants from Tokar in north-central Anatolia took over as the predominant vendors of simit which had previously been the purview of emigrants of Kastamonu.[56] The introduction of European Union norms for food safety and preparation further challenged the vendors' activities. They have to pay the government for a license and they have to display the simits behind glass windows instead of the commonly used open vehicles.[57]

Another typical street food for Istanbul is *kokoreç*. It consists of grilled lamb intestines wrapped around a core of skewered sweetbreads. Its origins are also linked to immigration. In

---

55. Defne Karaosmanoğlu, "Surviving the Global Market: Turkish Cuisine Under Construction," *Food, Culture and Society: An International Journal of Multidisciplinary Research* 12, no. 3 (2007), 437.

56. Alisa Roth, "Simit: Turkey's National Bread," *Gastronomica* 12, no. 4 (2012), 31ff.

57. Wißmann, "The Taste of a City," 37.

the middle of the twentieth century it arrived from the Balkans, specifically from Albania to Istanbul.[58]

Different forms of kebabs are also very common in Istanbul, in restaurants as well as on the streets. Other prepared meals sold for street consumption are *tavuk pilav* (rise with chickpeas and chicken), corn on the cob, and roasted chestnuts. Sweets like street taffy or drinks like fresh fruit juice are also offered. In the case of juice, the global influence can be observed in recent decades as exotic foreign fruits like coconut or pineapple have appeared alongside typical street drinks like orange juice.[59]

Popular with locals and tourists alike, fish sandwiches, so called *balik ekmek*, are sold in the area around the Galata bridge as well as all other areas near to the shore. The fish are roasted at fixed stalls or at mobile grills. Vendors regularly offer the sandwiches from anchored boats directly to the people walking on the riverside, like food trucks on water.[60] This gives the impression that the fish are regional and fresh which is not necessarily the case. Due to overfishing and pollution of the sea near the Turkish coast, the grilled fish are often frozen mackerel from Norway or Morocco.[61]

Despite the diversity and popularity of street food, vendors are decreasing in number in Istanbul. [62] The decrease remains unaffected by the growth of the city which is forecasted to reach twenty-three million inhabitants in ten years.[63]

---

58. Istanbul Eats, "Ali Usta Kokoreç: Gut Master," CulinaryBackstreest. com (blog), August 20, 2012, http://www.culinarybackstreets.com/istanbul/2012/ali-usta-kokorec/.

59. Wißmann, "The Taste of a City," 37.

60. Jonathan Wynn, "The Social Context behind Street Food: Authenticity, Culture and Ethnicity," Everyday Sociology (blog), September 29, 2014, http://www.everydaysociologyblog.com/2014/09/the-social-context-behind-street-food-authenticity-culture-and-ethnicity.html.

61. "Overfishing, pollution leave Turkish waters bare," *Hürriyet Daily News*, February 10, 2014, http://www.hurriyetdailynews.com/overfishing-pollution-leave-turkish-watersbare.aspx?pageID=238&nID=62272&NewsCatID=341.

62. Wißmann, "The Taste of a City," 37; and Kamrava, "The semi-formal," 68.

63. Enlil, "The Neoliberal," 22.

Conclusion

The globalization of Istanbul with its concomitant neoliberal economic policies, rapid growth in population, and integration of transnational networks has had a significant impact on the social formation as well as the urban geography of the biggest Turkish city. Istanbul once had a homogeneous middle-class character; however, the inequalities in income, wealth, and power have been growing since the 1980s.[64] Finding a job in the food sector was for many immigrants the only possibility to make a living.[65] This can be observed in many other urban centers worldwide, for instance, Los Angeles and Taipei.

Chain migration notoriously induces origin-dominated business controls as seen in the cases of midye dolma and simit vendors. The renovation of the Tarlabaşı district sheds light of the limited possibility for resistance from Kurdish street food businessmen. The vendors perceive themselves criminalized because of their origin and not their job. The example of the "Kurdish mussels" brings together the topics street food and migration as well as neo-liberal urban planning, marginalization, and the establishment of gentrified neighborhoods in a global city.

A limiting factor in writing this essay was my lack of Turkish language skills, and as such, many studies concerning street food and migration were not available in languages accessible to me. Due to geographical, time and resource constraints, a field study or survey was not possible for this paper. Another limitation is the informal nature of the selling of midye dolma. The area of Tarlabaşı is currently under construction, and the long-term consequences for the midye dolma vendors are not assessable. Each of these factors offers a point to delve deeper into the street food

---

64. Keyder, "Globalization and Social Exclusion in Istanbul," 124–25.
65. Gisèle Yasmeen, "Stockbrokers Turned Sandwich Vendors: The Economic Crisis and Small-scale Food Retailing in Southeast Asia," *Geoforum* 32 (2001): 91.

of Istanbul. While this article has provided a point of departure, there remains a wealth of potential research opportunities concerning Istanbul's street food and the vendors that make it their livelihood.

Bibliography

Anliamater, Iris. "Illegal Food Systems: Street Mussels in Istanbul." *TheMiracalOfFeedingCities.com* (blog), July 18, 2014, accessed January 7, 2015. http://miracleofeedingcities.com/illegal-food-systems-street-mussels-in-istanbul/.

Ates, Mustafa, Asli Ozkizilcik, and Cengiz Tabakoglu. "Microbiological Analysis of Stuffed Mussels Sold in the Streets," *Indian J Microbiology* 51, no. 3 (2011): 350–54.

Bingol, Enver Baris, Hilal Colek, Hamparsun Hampikyan, and Karlo Muratoglu. "The Microbiological Quality of Stuffed Mussels (Midye Dolma) sold in Istanbul," *British Food Journal* 110, no. 11 (2008): 1079–87.

Çelik, Aysun. "Binnenmigrationsbewegungen in der Türkei: Konstruierte regionale Beziehungen in der Migration". Diploma thesis, University of Vienna, 2009.

Dinçer, İclal. "The Impact of Neoliberal Policies on Historic Urban Space: Areas of Urban Renewal in Istanbul," *International Planning Studies* 16, no. 1 (2011): 43–60.

Endres, Clifford. "Edouard Roditi and the Istanbul Avant-Garde," *Texas Studies in Literature and Language* 54 No 4 (2012): 12.

Enlil, Zeynep Merey. "The Neoliberal Agenda and the Changing Urban Form of Istanbul," *International Planning Studies* 16, no. 1 (2011): 5–25.

Ergin, Murat. "The Racialization of Kurdish Identity in Turkey," *Ethnic and Racial Studies* 37 no. 2 (2014): 322–41.

Ferner, Manfred. *Istanbul und Umgebung: City Guide*. Bielefeld: Reise Know How Verlag Peter Rump, 2012.

Islam, Tolga. "Outside the Core. Gentrification in Istanbul." In *Gentrification in a Global Context: The new urban colonialism*, edited by Rowland Atkinson and Gary Bridge, 12–36. London and New York: Routledge, 2005.

Kamrava, Mehran. "The Semi-formal Sector and the Turkish Political Economy," *British Journal of Middle Eastern Studies* 31, no. 1 (2004): 63–87.

Karaosmanoğlu, Defne. "Surviving the Global Market. Turkish Cuisine Under Construction," *Food, Culture and Society: An International Journal of Multidisciplinary Research* 12, no. 3 (2007): 425–48.

Keyder, Caglar. "Globalization and Social Exclusion in Istanbul," *International Journal of Urban and Regional Research* 29, no. 1 (2005): 124–34.

MacDonald, John S., and Leatrice D. MacDonald. "Chain Migration Ethnic Neighborhood Formation and Social Networks," *The Milbank Memorial Fund Quarterly* 42, no. 1 (1964), 82–97.

Maier, Susanne. *Widerstand & Wäscheleinen: Stadterneuerung und räumliche Taktiken der Gegenkultur eines Vereins und seiner Akteurinnen in Tarlabaşı/Istanbul.* Diploma thesis, University of Vienna, 2010.

Mehveş, Konuk, and Yavuz Serpil. "Istanbul's Street Food Vendors, Municipal Officers Disagree on Regulations," *Hürriyet Daily News*, August 4, 2010. http://www.hurriyetdailynews.com/default.aspx-?pageid=438&n=streetside-vendors-and-municipality-officers-disagree-on-street-food-standards-2010-08-04.

Morley, David. "Istanbul tales: David Morley Reflects on the Past and Future of Istanbul," *Soundings* 37 (2007): 45–57.

Pamuk, Orhan. "Forbidden Fare." *The New Yorker*, July 9, 2007, 48.

Roth, Alisa. "Simit: Turkey's National Bread," *Gastronomica* 12, no. 4 (2012): 31–36.

Sağlam, Güliz. *Li Durî Malê / Evden Uzakta / Far Away From Home,* DVD, 2003, 29 min.

Sassen, Saskia. "The Global City: Introducing a Concept," *Brown Journal of World Affairs* 11, no. 2 (2005): 27–43.

Schmitt, Maggie. "Mussels on the Streets of Istanbul," *The Atlantic*, December 2, 2009. http://www.theatlantic.com/health/archive/2009/12/mussels-on-the-streets-of-istanbul/31058/.

Secor, Anna. "'There Is an Istanbul That Belongs to Me': Citizenship, Space, and Identity in the City," *Annals of the Association of American Geographers* 94, no. 2 (2004): 352–68.

Sonnenschein, Femke, and Toon van Meijl. "Migration and the Dialogue of Multiple Identifications: Kurdish Migrants in the Tourist Industry of Istanbul," *Identities: Global Studies in Culture and Power* 25, no. 5 (2014): 481–97.

Stanley, Bruce. "Istanbul." In *Cities of the Middle East and North Africa: A Historical Encyclopedia*, edited by Michael Dumper and Bruce Stanley, 180–88. Santa Barbara: ABC-Clio, 2007.

Steigemann, Renate, Hans E. Latzk, and Bernhard Weisser. *Istanbul*. Munich: Polyglott Verlag, 2001.

Turan, Neyran. "Towards an Ecological Urbanism for Istanbul." In *Megacities. Urban Form, Governance and Sustainability*, edited by André Sorensen, and Junichiro Okata, 223–43. Tokyo: Springer, 2011.

Wißmann, Katrin. "The Taste of a City," *Food Service Europe & Middle East* 1 (2010): 37.

Wynn, Jonathan. "The Social Context Behind Street Food: Authenticity, Culture and Ethnicity," *Everyday Sociology* (blog), September 29, 2014. http://www.everydaysociologyblog.com/2014/09/the-social-context-behind-street-food-authenticity-culture-and-ethnicity.html.

Yalcintan, Murat Cemal, and Adem Erdem Erbas. "Impacts of 'Gecekondu' on the Electoral Geography of Istanbul," *International Labor and Working-Class History* 64 (2003): 9–111.

Yasmeen, Gisèle. "Stockbrokers Turned Sandwich Vendors: The Economic Crisis and Small-scale Food Retailing in Southeast Asia," *Geoforum* 32 (2001): 91–102.

Norway`s Street Food on Wheels: Gourmet Food Trucks and Swedish Influence in Oslo

Kine Ariela Hemli

I decided to study street food with a focus on my home country, Norway. I did so not only because street food traditionally does not have a strong grip in Norway, but also to identify any possible new food experiences and challenges to the status quo in Norwegian culinary culture. To understand if this might be the case, I needed to develop a broader understanding of Norwegian identity in regards to food and food habits. What lies behind traditional Norwegian food culture? Moreover, what might be causing it to change?

Recently, the first gourmet food truck has arrived in Oslo with food prepared by a Michelin chef.[1] The chief postulate of this essay is that the food truck trend in Sweden presents opportunities for Norwegians to adapt to the idea of street food in general and, in particular, the internationally flavored gourmet food trucks in Oslo. I start with a brief overview of traditional Norwegian food and eating habits and then move on to my main discussion of how street food in Oslo is an obvious phenomenon of immigration of people and ideas. The time span will cover the 1960s up until today.

Norway is a relatively small country with a total of 5,109,000 inhabitants, and the focus of this essay will be on the largest city: Oslo.[2] When comparing Oslo to major urban centers such as Taipei,

---

1. Diner's Club International, Nordisk street food-turné, accessed November 18, 2015, http://www.dinersclub.no/street-food-by-diners-club/tab/tab-re/Street-food-i-Oslo-/.
2. Statistisk sentralbyrå, Folkemengde, January 2014, http://www.ssb.no/befolkning/statistikker/folkemengde.

Vienna, Istanbul, or London, Oslo is a small city with only 634,463 citizens.[3] This difference in size affects street food in Norway. The term "street food" relates to a relatively new concept in Norway.

In this article, I will provide examples of street foods in Norway. An important point to consider is that the Norwegian term for street food is *Gatemat* (*Gate* means street, *Mat* means food), however this is not actually street food as understood in this volume; the new street food is known in Norway by the English term "street food", which encompasses today's big food truck trend. It is used especially in news reports of the success of Swedish food truck business, which in one year has increased to thirty food trucks in Stockholm alone.[4] With Scandinavian brotherhood and identity in mind, the same trend may be initiated in Norway. The gourmet street food trend started about six years ago and is a further development from the more common, lower priced food trucks.[5]

America is the home of food trucks that have been serving up tasty treats for over two decades, showing that the basic concept is nothing new. Yet, the food truck has taken on new meaning as the mobile food industry continues to morph.[6] A brief overview of food-truck history will aid in understanding this development.

In concluding this paper, I discuss how the trends of street food in Norway nowadays are influenced by Swedish immigra-

---

3. Oslo Kommune, "Folkemengdens størrelse og sammensetning Oslo kommune," *Statistisk årbok for Oslo 2014*, December 1, 2014, http://statistisk-arbok.utviklings-og-kompetanseetaten.oslo.kommune.no/2014/id/UKE-2014-Kap00-3.

4. "Food trucks in Stockholm," accessed November 16, 2014, http://stockholmfoodtrucks.nu/; and Eirin Larsen, "Den hotteste maten skal spises stående," NRK online, November 8, 2014, http://www.nrk.no/rogaland/na-er-*gatemat*-blitt-hoykultur-1.12031196.

5. Alexandra Meyer, "The History of Gourmet Food Trucks," Yahoo7, April 18, 2012, accessed October 25, 2014, https://au.lifestyle.yahoo.com/food/index/article/-/13456587/the-history-of-gourmet-food-trucks.

6. Richard Myrick, "The Complete History of American Food Trucks," Mobile-Cuisine, accessed October 10, 2014, http://mobile-cuisine.com/business/history-of-american-food-trucks/.

tion and so-called Western trends. The result of this article is to provide an overview and status of Norwegian street food and to investigate whether there is a connection between Swedish street food activities and Norway`s street food, and by doing so, to fill the gap in the literature of this area.

The references used in this paper are internet sources and articles from the Norwegian University of Science and Technology. This research is based on a phenomenon in its very early stages in Norway, and is therefore unique. Due to this situation, very little literature regarding the topic is available. Using these resources provides information on Norwegian street food, combining well-documented aspects of traditional food, health, and nutrition with an observation of migration, which includes the migration of knowledge and ideas challenging status quo.

Traditional Norwegian Food and Eating Habits —a Historical Background

The historical studies of traditional Norwegian food done by Annechen Bahr Bugge contextualize current dinner eating by focusing on two periods: 1500–1940 and 1940–2006. This approach allows direct access to understanding what traditional Norwegian food and eating habits are.

The upper class has been at the forefront in adopting changes in food habits since the rich Viking chiefs up until now, with the urban middleclass now leading the way. There have always been changes in the Norwegian kitchen; however, these changes have been neither quick nor dramatic. This has to be viewed in connection with the fundamental conservatism that characterizes Norwegians' relationship to food. An example of how this manifests itself in the general skepticism towards new foods and dishes such as coffee, rice porridge, or frozen pizza.[7]

7· Annechen Bahr Bugge, *Å Spise Middag* (Trondheim: Tapir Akademisk Forlag, 2006), 57–58.

In the period between 1940–2006, modern Norwegian dinner recipes developed a more multicultural flair. Despite the introduction of many new ingredients, new dishes, and ways to cook and prepare existing dishes, there is nothing pointing to a decline of traditional dishes. The traditional plate-model still dominates Norwegian dinner tables. The plate-model consists of meat or fish (preferably minced) with steamed potatoes and vegetables.[8] Due to the fundamental conservatism mentioned above, the plate model might be one reason for why street food has not yet been accepted.

Aase Strømstad describes traditional foods such as *fenalår* (salted leg of lamb), ham, many kinds of smoked and salted meats served with potato salad, sour cream, and flatbread. These dishes display the influence of the logistics of food transportation without refrigeration. Today's eating habits are increasingly influenced by modern methods of preservation and freezing, and the import of foodstuffs from every corner of the world has completely changed the Norwegians' eating habits. Furthermore, Norwegians travel, are inspired by other food traditions, and tempted by unusual dishes while the same time remaining conscious of their own traditional food and food culture. After learning that fried foods are unhealthy, boiled meat and fish have again become popular. Strømstad describes how cured, salted, and smoked foods, *lefser*, and flatbread are served with pride to guests. Another typical Norwegian dish is "fish food," in which white fish such as haddock and wolffish are ground and made into fish balls, fish loaf, or fish patties.[9]

Health has always been a topic connected to food. According to Jensen and Kjærnes, Norway has a highly educated population with a good knowledge of both hygiene and nutrition. A survey from as early as the mid-1960s shows a high public

---

8. Bugge, *Å Spise Middag*, 31–99.

9. Aase Strømstad, *The Norwegian Kitchen* (Oslo: Boksenteret, 1999), accessed November 16, 2014, http://www.nb.no/nbsok/nb/0b24e615d07f3596f2c-5c1ef6504f35a?index=6#9.

interest and knowledge regarding nutrition, with the public becoming aware of the health problems associated with dietary fat. This strengthens the negative attitude towards the introduction of street food that tends towards cheaper preparation methods that rely on frying and batter.

Nutrition policy has a strong impact on daily life, habits, and private values in Norway. The Nordic welfare states were built on the strong influence of social-democratic political ideology, an ideology that links expertise with the state regulation of markets and individuals. In the midst of the Nordic welfare state system of the 1930s market disturbances, hunger, and war characteristics of liberal, market-based industrialism emerged, which created conditions for a strong government. Nutrition was presented and documented as an extensive social problem mainly linked to economic resources within families as well as a lack of knowledge and motivation. Nutrition, housing, and full employment became parameters in the macroeconomic models used in government planning. The goal was to influence the population towards "rational" dietary practices. This "rationality" was based on scientific knowledge: economics, nutrition, and "scientific household routines." For this goal to be met, transparency played a key role alongside access to nutritional information.

This presents a challenge for street food. Nutrition became "a good cause" and an instrument in directing consumption according to the needs of production interests. The government placed priority on state support for the production of foods that were both needed for health reasons in the working class and those supporting agriculture. The image of the "modern housewife" was closely linked to hygiene. Hygiene encompassed sickness prevention and health promotion. In this century, bacteriology and cleanliness have become important for linking individual health to social conditions and state responsibility. In their daily lives, consumers are caught between science and producer interests. Structures, bureaucracies, professions, and negotiated solutions change slowly. Market regulations are developing in new directions such as the European trend of the acceptance of a liberal market and international harmonization. These balanced out by providing consumers formal individual rights to protection and giving general guidelines in declarations on values like safety, information, and participation.

Today's strong consumer role in Norway is built on pluralistic activity patterns, making claims and alliances together with experts within a suitable ideological framework, and links between the modern consumer culture and the political system.[10] Observed from this historical perspective, there cannot be street food without immigration because it does not fit the indigenous eating culture.

Immigration's History and Impact on Norwegian Food

Before the contemporary immigration influx to Norway, Norwegian culture was seen as monolithic; however, minority groups in Norway have greatly contributed to the Norwegian culture. Twentieth-century immigration primarily occurred between 1960 and1970, when Norway needed workers and invited people from other countries—mainly Pakistan, Turkey, and Morocco. Since then, Norwegian culture has not only been folk songs, *bunad* (national costume) and other Norwegian traditions, but has also included food coming along with immigrants, especially the kebab. Many places selling kebab emerged, where Norwegians, Turks, Pakistanis, and others nationalities eat meals together. Indian and Chinese cuisines have also become very popular. The various dishes brought by immigrants have now become a part of the Norwegian culture.[11]

---

10. Thor Øivind Jensen and Unni Kjærnes "Designing the Good Life: Nutrition and Social Democracy in Norway," in *Constructing the New Consumer Society*, eds. Pekka Sulkunen, John Holmwood, Hilary Radner, and Gerhard Schulze (London: Macmillan Press, 2007), 218–33.
11. "Norsk kultur endrer seg med innvandring," *Kulturuttrykk – Kultur og språk* (blog), February 29, 2008, http://nlk1stc.wordpress.com/norsk-kultur/.

The 1980s significantly impacted the Norwegian food history. Chef and food-expert Magnus Tvedt-Øresland explains that before 1980, the term "housewife" was common, but during 1980s, more and more women started working outside of the home, to provide the family with a second income. An increased demand and need for simplification of the dishes and foods followed this, not only because there now was less time to cook and prepare food, but also due to the somewhat better economy and increased travel opportunities.

Travelling leads to more knowledge and curiosity for foods. A significant trend in 1985 was the rise of Chinese dishes. Tacos became the hip food at the end of the 1980s, and grilled chicken became Friday food easily obtained at the convenience store. Cheese, grapes, and wine became Saturday's "happy food." Pasta dishes, Mexican casseroles, and moussaka became popular. In 2014, the sale of tacos and pizza was higher than ever before.[12] The increased sale of non-traditional Norwegian foods testifies to a cultural shift, acceptance, and curiosity towards other food cultures. It creates a more receptive atmosphere towards street food, and an increased consciousness of one's own food traditions. Global trends, such as immigration, have created a multicultural Oslo. The amount of immigrants with cultural traditions of economic public food consumption creates a market for street food.

Sweden, Norway`s neighboring country, obtains its largest cultural influence externally. In 2013, six times as many asylum applications were accepted in Sweden compared to Norway. At the same time, Swedes make up one of the top ten immigrant populations by citizenship in Norway.[13] When Norway has had such

12. Silje Bjørnstad, "80-tallsmaten vi ikke glemmer," Side 2 online, accessed November 8, 2014, http://www.side2.no/helse/80-tallsmaten-vi-ikke-glemmer/8504930.html.
13. Lars Magne Sunnanå, "Innvandringspolitikken som ryster svensk politikk," *Aftenposten* online, September 15, 2014, http://www.aftenposten.no/nyheter/uriks/Innvandringsbolgen-som-ryster-svensk-politikk-7705983.html.

strong immigration, it has been geographically and commercially concentrated. More Norwegians rely on disability benefits, says the Norwegian Confederation of Trade Unions' chief economist Stein Reegård. Work immigration from Sweden pushes Norwegian youth out of the job market and increases housing prices.[14] This shows that Swedes exert some influence on Norwegian society.

Street Food in the Ambiguity Zone

As a Norwegian, I thought I knew what street food was. It had to be the street kitchens known as *gatekjøkken*. The issue with the understanding of *gatekjøkken* as street food, is that you can sit down. *Gatekjøkken* are colorful small locations with few chairs often in a tiny corner by the exit with a toilet always within or nearby. As such, *gatekjøkken* can be understood to be closer to restaurants and take-away establishments.

Examples of street foods in Norway draw inspiration from Peru, Korea, Mexico, and the United States and apply it to *gatemat* in trendy restaurants. In news articles, street food and *gatemat* are often used side by side as in this headline of an article online: "We wish to collect different types of *gatemat*, street food, in this restaurant".[15]

Pulled pork, pulled chicken, grilled tapas, bread and focaccia baked on the grill, stuffed grilled paprika, and skewers with beef mixed with Mexican, Indian or Asian flavors are some of what you can get at Mathallen.[16] Mathallen is one of the best examples of *gatemat* in Oslo. It is a center for food culture in Oslo

---

14. Tore Tollersrud, Sporstøl Ellen, and Svein Vestrum Olsson, "LO: Svensker presser ut norsk ungdom," NRK online, March 5, 2013, http://www.nrk.no/norge/lo-frykter-svensk-innvandring-1.10935807.

15. Erik Gulbrandsen, "Gatemat i mathallen," *Aftenposten* online, March 11, 2014, http://www.aftenposten.no/osloby/sulten/Gatemat-i-Mathallen-94512b.html

16. Ragnhild Kolvereid and Anette Fjelleng Hansen, "Tøff og trendy gatemat," Matprat online, accessed December 9, 2014, http://www.matprat.no/artikler/tema/toff-og-trendy-gatemat/.

where you can purchase high-quality products from Norwegian small-scale producers and special foreign imports. The retro trend now favors locally produced foods which are regarded as the finest food mixed with exotic flavors.[17]

According to Tommy Raanati, general manager at the Gastronomisk Institutt (gastronomical institute), street food is the hottest trend in Europe right now, and Norway is a bit slow but is coming along.[18] He says street food should look nice, be flavorful with different ingredients, healthy, and quick and easy to make. The most important part is that it should taste exceptional and have the ability to replace foods like kebab and hamburgers. The trendiest foods are meant to be eaten standing. Raanati says he waits in anticipation to see who takes the leap and tries to make it with a real food truck.

Food Trucks

Food trucks are a well-known phenomenon in many American and British cities. As the embodiment of street food on wheels, food trucks sit at the intersection of an entrepreneurial spirit and the challenges of contemporary economic realities. Because of high rents and requirements for start-up money in the restaurant business, a subculture of food truckers started to emerge especially during the economic crises of 2008. The trucks are built as mobile kitchens, where the food is served fresh to the customers waiting outside. It is a myth that there is a lot of money in the food truck business. You have to to have a twist and be unique.[19] Just as in Providence, USA, 140 years ago, where the first food truck started

---

17. "Mathallen Food Hall," Visit Oslo online travel guide, accessed January 6, 2015, http://www.visitoslo.com/en/activities-and-attractions/shopping/?TLp=583195&Mathallen-Food-Hall#product-info1.

18. Larsen, "Den hotteste maten skal spises stående."

19. "Food trucks och matvagnar," Foodjunkies website, accessed November 16, 2014, http://foodjunkies.se/food-trucks-och-matvagnar/.

its business, the food-truck operators tried to keep their prices low while setting themselves apart with a signature dish.[20]

The trend has grown with technology to the point that people can now track their favorite truck online and follow them to food truck parties and festivals.[21] In 2010, The US government added "Tips for Starting Your Own Street Food Business" to its small business website.[22] In November 2010, Los Angeles started ranking Food Trucks with grades like restaurants.[23]

Startup—Food Trucks in Norway

It is clear that the term "street food" is flexible; however, some indications are pointing to the re-establishment of the use of the term "street food" after being a concept negatively associated with many littering problems in Oslo, when it then was closely related to fast food. In 2007, the Oslo municipality decided that they would stop accepting these food trucks and stands, allowing only one food truck to stay after this, in Youngstorget. Now it is changing, and the laws are easing up, with the focus on making new rules in the summer of 2015.[24]

---

20. Daniel Engber, "Who Made That Food Truck?," *The New York Times Magazine* online: May 2, 2014. http://www.nytimes.com/2014/05/04/magazine/who-made-that-food-truck.html?_r=1.

21. Kyle. "Food Truck Tracker," Food truck Fiesta website, accessed October 25, 2014, http://foodtruckfiesta.com/; Allison Saunders, "Yes, we're throwing a Food Truck Party," *The Coast* online, July 18, 2014, http://www.the-coast.ca/RestaurantandBarNews/archives/2014/07/18/yes-were-throwing-a-food-truck-party; and Samantha Stanich, "Food Truck Festival a Success," *Times Leader* online, October 20, 2014, http://timesleader.com/news/features/50528567/Food-Truck-Festival-a-success.

22. NicoleD, "Tips for Starting Your Own Street Food Business," U.S. Small Business Administration, September 21, 2010, http://www.sba.gov/blogs/tips-starting-your-own-street-food-business.

23. Myrick, "The Complete History of American Food Trucks."

24. Karl Martin Jakobsen "Nå inntar mat-truckene Oslo," *Aftenposten* online, November 7, 2014, http://www.aftenposten.no/osloby/Na-inntar-mat-truckene-Oslo-75021b.html.

Even street food (Gatemat) creates headlines such as the following "Gatemat on wheels to Oslo citizens".[25] This article is about a food truck unlike former food trucks. It serves high quality, local food prepared by a professional chief. The truck does not yet have a place to park, but in the meantime, they serve street food to customers on *Gaasa* in Oslo (a café/pub) three days a week. Svein-Erik Hilsen is not the only chef pursuing the food truck concept. Celebrity chef Ole Martin Alfsen and restaurant entrepreneur Stian Floer started up the first food truck in the country in May 2014, in connection with the food festival, *Taste for Everyone*. In the same month, a food truck with Norwegian sea food started up and was on the road by the Norse sea. Michelin-chef Even Ramsvik cooked *gatemat* from a truck during the event *Street food by Diners Club* held in September the same year. As Hilsen says, it is good that more and more people are becoming interested in street food and food trucks. It has caused the Norwegian department of business to work on where to put the trucks in order for the food to spread more throughout the city.

Gourmet

This new trend started about six years ago and is a further development with finer food than that of the common, low-priced food trucks. This gourmet trend evolved to the point in the USA that it inspired things like the annual Vendy Awards, which celebrate the best in mobile food achievements, Street Food Vending classes in NYC, for those who want to become mobile food vendors, food truck cookbooks, reality shows, and much more. The food trucks would never have taken off like they did without the help social media. The use of Facebook and Twitter to track the

---

25. Trine Dahl Johansen, "Gatemat på hjul til Oslofolket," *Nettavisen* online, August 26, 2014, http://www.dittoslo.no/indre-by/nyheter-indre-by/*gatemat*-pa-hjul-til-oslofolket-1.8559425.

trucks, advertise specials of the day or explaining new menu items helped food trucks grow into a culinary phenomenon.[26]

Food Trucks in Sweden

The phenomenon of street food has spread in Stockholm, growing rapidly to around thirty food trucks in the past year.[27] The biggest difference between the American food trucks and the Swedish—and soon Norwegian—food trucks are the higher prices per meal serving, earlier closing times, and strict hygiene regulations. The range of food trucks with international dishes includes the Turkish themed Köftebilen truck, El Taco Truck with the staple Mexican offerings, and the clearly named Indian Street Food. The food described above in Mathallen, are foodstuff concepts based on similarly styled Swedish food trucks.[28] In 2013, the Swedish municipality of Stockholm allowed food trucks as an experiment, after pressure from street food enthusiasts. They are monitoring it closely, due to earlier problems with hygiene and the environment.[29] This trend generates a new revenue stream, which, as Swedish news now says, can boost tourism.[30]

It appears street food is being revived in a new direction than earlier attempts such as *gatemat*. Now, street food—with more focus on better foods, earlier closing times, better hygiene, famous chefs, and repeated reporting on the Swedish success— spreads in food trucks in Norway.

---

26. Meyer, "The History of Gourmet Food Trucks."
27. Jakobsen "Nå inntar mat-truckene Oslo."
28. "Food trucks in Stockholm."
29. Linda Bock, "Food trucks sprider sig över Stockholms gator," SVT Nyheter, August 10, 2013, http://www.svt.se/nyheter/sverige/food-trucks-pa-rull-i-stockholm.
30. Mats Berggren, "Food trucks kan lyfta turismen," *Besöksli* online, July 31, 2013, http://www.besoksliv.se/artikel/food-trucks-kan-lyfta-turismen-34895.

Designing the Future—Who Takes the Lead and Who Follows?

Innovation has become a buzzword that is used in many contexts. It shows that we are increasingly interested in change and in the creation of newness. It is, moreover, a focus on new technologies and ways of thinking, as this can be the foundation for new companies or securing the profitability of existing ones.

The process of measuring innovation and comparing companies and countries is no easy task. One method is to measure the scope of research and development work (FoU). In 2007 Norway used 1.64 percent of its gross domestic product (GDP) on FoU, which equals 900 euro per citizen, a value lower than Sweden. In 2006, the amount of innovation enterprises in Norway was estimated to 35.5 percent, and in Sweden, that number was 44.6 percent. If we, on the other hand, only look at GDP, the story differs: Norway is far ahead of the innovation-leader Sweden.[31] This larger trend reflects the situation for food trucks where issues in Norway exist primarily at the political level, which limits investment while Sweden is leading in food truck innovation.[32]

Trends

The current eating trend in Norway is young adults taking back the traditional foods that the 1980s and 1990s left behind. Many traditional dishes lost popularity around that time, and have gradually disappeared from dinner tables. Now these traditional dishes such as fresh meat and meatballs are reappearing, says Magnus Tvedt-Øresland.[33]

---

31. K.H. Sørensen, "Det norske samfunn – et innovasjonssystem?," *Det norske samfunn*, no.6 (2010), 67–90.

32. Jakobsen "Nå inntar mat-truckene Oslo."

33. Bjørnstad, "80-tallsmaten vi ikke glemmer."

According to a 2007 press release from Statens Institutt for Forbruksforskning (SIFO—Norway's institute for consumer research), it is reported that during the last 30 years, there has been a threefold increase in the costs of dining at restaurants, bars, and similar establishments. Nine out of ten Norwegians have eaten out during the last two months, with younger people eating out more frequently than the older population, and people in Oslo eating out more frequently compared to the rest of the country.

SIFO says the attraction of food from other countries is strongly featured in the eating habits of this decade. Gas stations, fast food restaurants, kiosks and taverns are establishments of low cultural status. Two central trends in dining-out: increased interest in healthy foods and culinary experiences. Sushi is an example of a dish that is becoming increasingly popular. Consumers want fast food, but not junk food. Youth, the most active group eating out, are demanding Italian, American, and Mexican food. Adults, on the other hand, tend to choose gourmet, ethnic, or informal restaurants, and the elderly more often choose to eat at patisseries or cafes.[34]

Even though Norwegians now eat out more than before, reports from SIFO show that the majority of meals are eaten at home and that eating out is no threat to family meals. Food and dishes appear to have reached a higher status and are receiving increased interest. Dining out is not only focused on the food, but romance, flirting, pleasure, self-representation, and the social experience, as dining out is rarely done alone.[35]

The selection of restaurants has changed radically during the last decade. In 1963, Oslo saw the opening of La Petite Cuisine, followed by Peking House in 1969, and the first Peppes Pizza in 1970. Since then, at a time when bell peppers were considered foreign and not recognized by many Norwegians, today, 76

---

34. Statens Institutt for Forbruksforskning, "Vi spiser ute som aldri før, "press release, 2007, accessed 16.11.14, http://www.sifo.no/files/file71777_utespise.pdf.
35. Statens Institutt for Forbruksforskning, "Vi spiser ute som aldri før."

percent of the population say they enjoy foreign foods, especially young adults between twenty-five and thirty-nine years of age. 56 percent want to avoid eating at gas stations, and fifty-two per cent avoid eating at kiosks. Both of which are places where the food is unhealthy, not generally enjoyed, too expensive, and does not taste as good as other establishments.[36] Food culture is popular, and unhealthy food is becoming less popular.

Conclusion

In the process of writing this essay, I expected to find out that migration, especially Swedish migration due to the Scandinavian culture being something familiar, would play a key role in influencing the acceptance of street food in Oslo.

The population's perception of street food and their own food habits are clearly influenced by individual identity, traditional Norwegian history and culture. Economic and political growth since the 1930s has promoted increasing awareness of hygiene and nutrition, which is reflected in the modern consumers actions.

In the analysis, I found, as expected, that immigration to Norway, which started in the 1960s, had challenged the Norwegian food heritage, and that street food is not widely available in Norway. It became clear that Norwegians have to be seen in connection with a fundamental conservatism concerning food and general skepticism towards new foods and dishes. Due to this, the media uses "big brother" Sweden's food truck success story as a method to aid the adoption of food trucks, as they are well aware that Sweden is leading in innovation that challenges the status quo. As shown, bureaucracies, professions and other systems are changing and adapting slowly, but are increasingly challenged by the

---

36. Tove Diesen, Josefin Engström and Jon-Are Berg-Jacobsen, "Vi spiser ute som aldri før," *Aftenposten* online, last modified October 12, 2011, http://www. aftenposten.no/fakta/innsikt/Vi-spiser-ute-som-aldri-for-5107441.html.

new European market regulations and consumer demographics. Early training of housewives by the state, and hesitant consumers have been key factors to why junk food was rejected. Traditional Norwegian foods and dishes prevail and remain the leading trend.

This essay has shown that, due to immigration and tourism, the Norwegian changes in food habits and views on new ethnic dishes have led to an increased acceptance of new flavors, ways to eat, and knowledge on food preparation.

The rather small population of the geographically long and thin country is kept well updated by a strong media and influenced by immigration from many countries, including Sweden. Because of this Swedish influence, Norwegian attitudes towards street food are softening up to give it another chance. Street food and food trucks are common in the USA and Europe for a long time, however it is only since the success of food trucks from Sweden that Norway has opened its eyes toward this trend. The idea of street food is already challenging the status quo of the typical foreigner food habit of getting "ready to go" food in a northern country of Scandinavia. From this and SIFO's research, it is evident that a market for street food does exist in Norway. It seems as if there is increasing acceptance of street food as a result of the use of the English term, "street food," and also that it maintains the traditions of locally produced food.

The current trends focus on quickly prepared food, locally produced but with exotic flavors, foreign dish presentation styles, and ideas of environmental health and hygiene. Gourmet food prepared by celebrity chefs and local food is exciting for the Norwegian population, who have experienced a culinary renaissance, demonstrated by the increasing popularity of dining out among Norwegians in the last decade.

In Norway, food trucks are in their initial phase, and they are challenging the status quo in every way on the small—almost non-existent—street food market. As street food is so new, it will be exciting to see what knowledge, ideas, and patterns will enter the market.

Bibliography

Berggren, Mats. "Food trucks kan lyfta turismen," *Besöksli* online, July 31, 2013. http://www.besoksliv.se/artikel/food-trucks-kan-lyfta-turismen-34895.

Bock, Linda. "Food trucks sprider sig över Stockholms gator," SVT Nyheter, August 10, 2013. http://www.svt.se/nyheter/sverige/food-trucks-pa-rull-i-stockholm.

Bjørnstad, Silje. "80-tallsmaten vi ikke glemmer," Side 2 online. Accessed November 8, 2014. http://www.side2.no/helse/80-tallsmaten-vi-ikke-glemmer/8504930.html.

Bugge, Annechen Bahr. *Å spise middag.* Trondheim: Tapir Akademisk Forlag, 2006.

D., Nicole. "Tips for Starting Your Own Street Food Business." U.S. Small Business Administration, September 21, 2010. http://www.sba.gov/blogs/tips-starting-your-own-street-food-business.

Diesen, Tove, Joesfin Engström, and Jon-Are Berg-Jacobsen. "Vi spiser ute som aldri før," *Aftenposten* online, last modified October 12, 2011. http://www.aftenposten.no/fakta/innsikt/Vi-spiser-ute-som-aldri-for-5107441.html.

Engber, Daniel. "Who Made That Food Truck?" *The New York Times Magazine* online, May 2, 2014. http://www.nytimes.com/2014/05/04/magazine/who-made-that-food-truck.html?_r=0.

Gulbrandsen, Erik. "Gatemat i mathallen,"*Aftenposten* online, March 11, 2014. http://www.aftenposten.no/osloby/sulten/Gatemat-i-Mathallen-94512b.html.

Jakobsen, Karl Martin. "Nå inntar mat-truckene Oslo," *Aftenposten* online, November 7, 2014. http://www.aftenposten.no/osloby/Na-inntar-mat-truckene-Oslo-75021b.html.

Jensen, Thor Øivind, and Unni Kjærnes. "Designing the Good Life: Nutrition and Social Democracy in Norway." In *Constructing the New Consumer Society*, edited by Pekka Sulkunen, John Holmwood, Hilary Radner, and Gerhard Schulze. London: Macmillan Press, 1997.

Johansen, Trine Dahl. "Gatemat på hjul til Oslofolket." *Nettavisen* online, August 26, 2014. http://www.dittoslo.no/indre-by/nyheter-indre-by/*gatemat*-pa-hjul-til-oslofolket-1.8559425.

Kolvereid, Ragnhild, and Anette Fjelleng Hansen. "Tøff og trendy gatemat." Matprat online. Accessed December 9, 2014. http://www.matprat.no/magasinet/sommer-2013/inspirasjon/toff-og-trendy-*gatemat*/.

Larsen, Eirin. "Den hotteste maten skal spises stående," NRK Rogaland online, November 8, 2014. http://www.nrk.no/rogaland/naer-*gatemat*-blitt-hoykultur-1.12031196.

Oslo Kommune. "Folkemengdens størrelse og sammensetning Oslo kommune." *Statistisk årbok for Oslo 2014*, December 1, 2014. http://statistisk-arbok.utviklings-og-kompetanseetaten.oslo.kommune.no /2014/id/UKE-2014-Kap00-3.

Saunders, Allison. "Yes, we're throwing a Food Truck Party." *The Coast* online, July 18, 2014. http://www.thecoast.ca/RestaurantandBarNews/archives/2014/07/18/yes-were-throwing-a-food-truck-party.

Sørensen, K.H. "Det norske samfunn – et innovasjonssystem?" *Det norske samfunn*, no. 6 (2010): 67-90.

Stanich, Samantha. "Food Truck Festival a Success." *Times Leader* online, October 20,2014. http://timesleader.com/news/features/50528567/Food-Truck-Festival-a-success.

Strømstad, Aase. *The Norwegian kitchen*. Oslo: Boksenteret, 1999. Accessed November 16, 2014. http://www.nb.no/nbsok/nb/0b24e615d07f3596f2c5c1ef6504f35a?index=6#9.

Sunnanå, Lars Magne. "Innvandringspolitikken som ryster svensk politikk," *Aftenposten* online, September 15, 2014. http://www.aftenposten.no/nyheter/uriks/Innvandringsbolgen-som-ryster-svensk-politikk-7705983.html.

Tollersrud, Tore, Ellen Sporstøl, and Svein Vestrum Olsson. "LO: Svensker presser ut norsk ungdom," NRK online, March 5, 2013. http://www.nrk.no/norge/lo-frykter-svensk-innvandring-1.10935807.

Sichuan-flavored Beef Noodle Soup in Taipei: Its Origin and Process of Becoming Popular in Taiwan

Wang Jin

As a Sichuanese, it is really interesting for me to see Taiwanese, Sichuan-flavored beef noodle soup in almost all the major cities in China. In Taipei, Sichuan-flavored beef noodle soup is one of the most famous street foods. Yet the origin of this typical Taiwanese street food actually does not come from the native Taiwanese. So where does this beef noodle soup originally come from? What is the connection of it to Chinese immigrants that came together with the Kuomintang government after World War II? When probing into the eating habits of native Taiwanese, one might wonder how beef noodle soup could have enjoyed such a high popularity in Taipei, as most native Taiwanese did not have the general habit of eating beef when WWII ended. Therefore, what is the process of general acceptance of beef in Taipei? Does it also contribute to the increasing popularity of beef noodle soup in Taipei? In the meantime, what is the role of governmental regulations on street food in Taipei? Has it also somehow helped beef noodle soup to prosper as street food over the decades? These questions will be the main focus of this short essay on beef noodle soup in Taipei.

In regard to sources on beef noodle soup in Taipei, I have consulted journal articles, news reports, personal blogs, books, governmental regulations from mainland China and Taiwan. Based on these sources, I started my research with the period of large-scale Chinese immigration after WWII and explore how Chinese immigrants have influenced local street food in Taipei; in my case, how Sichuan-flavored beef noodle soup in Taipei came into being. Researching the influence from the economy and culture of Taiwan after WWII on the beef eating among Taiwanese provided me with information about why some native Taiwanese did/do not eat beef. Then I went through the analysis on the governmental policies and regulations on street vendors so as to find out how these regulations help beef noodle soup to survive and prosper in the streets of Taipei.

Basically this essay is divided into three parts: the emergence of the street food beef noodle soup itself, the process of acceptance by Taiwanese people, and related governmental measures.

There have been a number of journal articles in China and Taiwan dealing with the origin of beef noodle soup in Taiwan. Yet the general research in this field done in Chinese is not comprehensive enough to explore the origin of this street food in detail. This essay is based on these research contributions but is written with a multi-faceted approach.

For future research on how Taiwanese gourmet culture and street food has contributed to Taiwan's tourism, this essay might help other researchers to find out how at least one typical Taiwanese street food came to the streets in Taipei and has attracted tourists from all around the world to sample it.

Beef Noodle Soup Made in Taiwan?

When one searches for beef noodle soup in Chinese "牛肉面" on a Google map of Taipei (Figure 1), she or he will definitely be amazed at how many spots s/he can actually go for a bowl of beef noodle soup in Taipei!

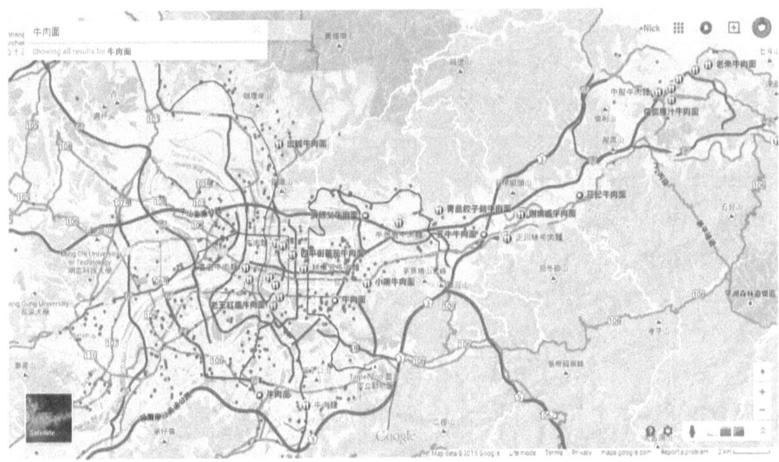

Figure 1. Search Result of "牛肉面 niurou mian" on Google map of Taipei, October 2014

What does this mean? It is safe to say that beef noodle soup is one of the most representative foods in Taipei, not only in restaurants, but also as cheap street food ubiquitous in Taipei.

While Taiwanese president Ma Ying-jeou was still mayor of Taipei, in order to promote beef noodle soup, he initiated the first Taipei International Beef Noodle Soup Festival in 2005, claiming that "the capital of beef noodle soup in the world is Taipei".[1] Beef noodle soup is basically divided into two different flavors in Taipei: one is non-spicy with clear soup and the other one is usually labeled as "Sichuan-flavored" due to its characteristic of being spicy. Sichuan-flavored beef noodle soup is more classic and representative due to its general popularity. This begs the question: is this Sichuan-flavored beef noodle soup really authentic and made in Taiwan? Where exactly does the dish come from?

---

1. Yang Mengyu, "A Message from Taiwan: 'King of Beef Noodle Soup' in Taipei," BBC Chinese News, November 29, 2006, Accessed January 1, 2015, http://news.bbc.co.uk/chinese/simp/hi/newsid_6120000/newsid_6120700/6120790.stm.

To address these questions, one has to go back to when the Kuomintang (Chinese Nationalist Party) was defeated by the China Communist Party during the civil war that broke out after WWII. According to the first census of Taiwan, around 1950 about 1.2 million Chinese emigrated together with the Kuomintang government from Mainland China to Taiwan. Among these Chinese immigrants, many soldiers and their family members came together to Taiwan as well. The family members of these soldiers lived in a community called a "military dependents' village."

To find out the actual origin of current Beef noodle soup, one has to move from North Taiwan to South Taiwan, a place called Gangshan(岡山). It is a suburban district in Kaohsiung City. Gangshan is where the Republic of China Air Force Academy is located, which relocated from Chengdu, the capital city of Sichuan Province in Mainland China. Many family members of these soldiers and officers from the Air Force lived in the military dependents' village of Gangshan. Most of them were actually from Sichuan.

At the time, the Kuomintang army was provided with supplies by the U.S. government, and senior officers that came from Mainland China with the Kuomintang government could get canned beef that was also allocated to the American army. To Chinese officers that came from Sichuan, who were used to their own taste of food, this foreign canned beef was not really delicious. They therefore accumulated a lot of these beef cans at home.

These officers knew that their chance of going back to their homeland was quite slim, but still they missed home and food that reminded them of home. Some of them therefore tried to plant chili peppers in Gangshan so that they would be able to make some Doubanjiang (bean segments sauce), which is believed to be "the soul in Sichuan cuisine."[2] Of course, what these

---

2. "Soul of Sichuan Cuisine," Apple Daily website, June 19, 2014, accessed January 2, 2015, http://hk.apple.nextmedia.com/supplement/food/art/20140619/18762363.

Sichuan officers made out of the chili peppers grown in the soil of Taiwan could never be compared to the most famous Doubanjiang from Pixian County in Chengdu, so they did a little experiment with the Doubanjiang by cooking the canned beef with the Doubanjiang that they prepared. Then they added some cooked noodles into the beef soup and in the end it did not taste bad, which somehow made these Sichuan officers feel at home food wise. To cook Sichuan-flavored beef noodle soup, one has to use this spicy Doubanjiang and therefore it is very likely that the origin of the very first Sichuan-flavored beef noodle soup came from Gangshan, according to Taiwanese historian Lu Yaodong.[3] This leads to another question: how does this beef noodle soup migrate to Taipei and become popular there?

Some of the soldiers that came together with the Kuomintang government no longer served in the army, and they had no other specific skills with which they could make a living. Yet they still remembered how their food tasted at home and knew how to prepare it. In order to survive, they started to make beef noodle soup and sold it in the streets of Taipei.

Taipei, as the capital of Taiwan, is the island's most populated city. Many young people came from the rural areas to this metropolis to seek for a better life. However, food in proper restaurants of Taipei seemed to be too expensive for these poor young people from the rural areas as well as for the students in Taipei. Therefore, cheap street food became the favorite food for them. They frequented street stands at Taipei Station, Ximending neighborhood, and Chien-Cheng Circle, and beef noodle soup became one of their favorite street foods.

Beef noodle soup in Taipei, most of the time also labeled with "authentic Sichuan flavor", can be misleading in its name

---

3. Lu Yaodong, "Where Does Beef Noodle Come From?" Taipei Beef Noodle Festival, October 12, 2005, accessed January 3, 2015, http://www.tbnf.com.tw/m_know.htm.

and makes tourists assume that it actually originates from Sichuan of mainland China. Such an assumption is wrong and right in some sense as this dish was invented by Sichuan immigrants to Taiwan, and it is truly made in Taiwan. Both Taiwanese and Chinese are sometimes wondering the origin of this typical Taiwanese street food, so they go to Sichuan or Taipei to try each other's beef noodle soup. In the end, they find out the flavors of beef noodle soup in Sichuan and Taipei nowadays are indeed different and cannot be claimed to be the same. As Luo Shengqing, the owner of the famous "Yung Kang Beef Noodle" in Taipei put it, "Sichuan-flavored beef noodle soup in Sichuan tastes totally different from the one in Taiwan."[4]

Beef Eating Habit of the Taiwanese: Taboo and Popularity

It goes without saying that beef noodle soup is now one of the most representative street foods of Taiwan. However, when one tries to examine the eating habits of native Taiwanese, s/he will be surprised to find out that in the 1950s beef eating was not popular at all when beef noodle soup conquered the streets of Taipei. Then how could beef noodle soup become increasingly popular and accepted by the Taiwanese?

In 1952 the agricultural sector of Taiwan contributed to 35.9 percent of Taiwan's GDP, and there were many people who were working in this sector, especially in southern Taiwan.[5] To these Taiwanese people, cattle were indispensable for their daily work in the fields and made a significant contribution to the ag-

---

4. "40 Years Non-stop Business of Taiwanese Beef Noodle Soup Plans Its Marketing in Mainland China," NET EASE, September 1, 2010, Accessed January 2, 2015, http://news.163.com/10/0901/09/6FG42A50000146BD .html?f=jsearch.

5. Jianfeng Xu, "Analysis of Change in Industrial Structure of Taiwan," *Taiwan Studies* 3 (2001): 56–63.

ricultural production. Taiwanese farmers saw cattle as their most loyal friends and part of their family. Out of economic necessity, respect, and gratitude, many farmers would never eat beef.

After the end of WWII, the spread of Buddhism was against the religion polices of China Communist Party and also due to the outbreak of the civil war, more and more Buddhists went to Taiwan to do missionary work there. The influence of Buddhism has historically played an important role in the culture of the Han Chinese, and Buddhism has been well preserved in Taiwan ever since the early immigration of Han Chinese during the Ming and Qing dynasties. According to the 2009 report on religious freedom from the U.S. State Department, 35 percent of Taiwanese identify themselves as Buddhists.[6] Then what is the relation between these facts and beef eating among Taiwanese?

When Buddhism was established in India, it incorporated some of the doctrines of Brahmanism. The divinity of cattle was therefore also part of Buddhism. One can find many stories about cattle and Buddha, which were depicted in the novels of the Ming and Qing dynasties. For instance, in the works of Ji Yun, a notable writer in Qing Dynasty, he told a Buddhist story, in which a bull knelt down to a butcher with tears in its eyes, begging for life. Yet the butcher was such a hard-hearted person and killed the bull anyway. Finally, the butcher ended up being cooked in a big wok together with the bull that he killed.[7]

Another influence from Buddhism is the concept of reincarnation. There is one expression in Chinese called "I would work as a horse or a bull for you in my next life(来世给你做牛做马lai shi gei ni zuo niu zuo ma)" which actually means to slave for some-

---

6. "Report on International Religious Freedom," U.S. Department of State, October 26, 2009, http://www.state.gov/documents/organization/132869.pdf.

7. Yan Han, "Punishment for Butcher for Killing a Bull That Begs for Life," Buddhist Network of Xingtai, November 11, 2014, http://www.xtfj.org/xuefu/fujiaogushi/20140911/20780.html.

body to pay his/her debt of gratitude. Reincarnation has played an important role in the culture of the Han Chinese, no matter if they actually believe in Buddhism or not. In the understanding of Buddhists, those who work for you as cattle were actually human beings who committed bad deeds or owed someone a big debt of gratitude in their previous life. They therefore reincarnate as cattle to pay their debt in this life. For this reason, cattle enjoy more divinity compared to other livestock among Taiwanese Buddhists.

Given this background, beef eating was not popular and sometimes was regarded as taboo among native Taiwanese. When did this start to change?

From the 1950s onwards, Taiwan experienced the mechanization of agricultural production and in 1991 the machinery operation rate for rice production achieved 100 percent.[8] A large amount of new agricultural equipment was imported to increase the agricultural production. As a result, the number of cattle used for agriculture decreased substantially. Since there was no more need for cattle for the field-work, the excessive cattle in agriculture went subsequently to the beef market. In the meantime, with the change of the industrial structure in Taiwan, more and more of the workforce of rural areas flew to the urban areas. Gradually these former farmers adopted the lifestyle in the cities and their eating habits were no exception. They began to accept more choices for their food, including beef.

From 1975, in order to control the ever-increasing price of Taiwanese beef in the market, the Taiwanese government opened the market for imported beef, mainly from Australia, New Zealand, and the U.S.[9] As the price for beef was under governmen-

8. Yikuan Li, "The Statue Quo and Development Trend of Agricultural Mechanization in Taiwan," website for Promotion of Agricultural Machinery in Guangdong Province, May 30, 2008, http://www.gdnjtg.com/view.php?news_ID=90&channel_ID=6&subject_ID=16.

9. Shan He, "Taiwan Opens the Beef Import from Canada for the Negotiations of TPP," Hong Kong China News Agency, January 17, 2014, http://www.hkcna.hk/content/2014/0117/238417.shtml.

tal control and the income of the Taiwanese became higher, the more ordinary Taiwanese could afford to eat out. Meanwhile, more street vendors began to sell beef noodle soup. Compared to the price of steak offered in a fancy Western restaurant, beef noodle soup obviously enjoyed more popularity among the general Taiwanese population.

Last but not the least, as military service for men has been compulsory in Taiwan since 1949, all men, no matter if they are from the South or the North, urban or rural areas, have to accept the food in the army during their time of service. The meat offered in military catering is mainly beef. Even though sometimes the varieties of food might not look satisfying, meat is always offered for lunch and supper, either pork or beef. Beef noodle soup could also often be seen at the street stands close to the barracks. To these soldiers, beef has become one of the most ordinary foods in their military life.

Governmental Regulation and Protection for Street Food

Beef noodle soup as a street food could not have survived and become so popular in Taipei if the Taiwanese government did not tolerate it in the beginning and even made relevant regulations to protect and promote it.

During the 1950s, many immigrants came to Taiwan from China. As there were not sufficient work opportunities for them, they started to make their living as street vendors. At that time, the Taiwanese government regarded it as a way to solve the unemployment of these immigrants. Hence, these street vendors were well tolerated by the government.

Starting from 1970s, as the industrial structure began to change, even more people decided to move from the rural areas into cities to seek for better life. Many among them were barely educated and did not possess professional skills to find a good job. During this period of time, the number of street vendors increased significantly and also brought a series of problems in the cities. Yet the unregulated trade did provide the very basic means for poor people to survive, so the Taiwanese government did not intervene and simply left them alone. The acquiescence of the government led to a further increase of street vendors.

By the 1980s, street vendors could already be seen everywhere in the cities and street vending was no longer a trade associated with lower socioeconomic status. In the meantime, street vending, according to the shops in the same areas of street vendors, posed some unfair competition. As a response to the protest of these shops, the Taiwanese government implemented a series of policies to solve the issues of street vending, such as establishing a closed street market to contain street vendors, and planning of relevant governmental regulations.

In 1999, a series of official regulations were announced by the Taiwanese government to regulate and protect street vending. The night markets in Taipei, where you can find all sorts of delicious street foods from most of the East-Asian and Southeast-Asian countries, developed into one of the most famous tourist attractions. Their existence is due to the tolerance and protection of the Taiwanese government as it became apparent that street vending has become an integral part of Taiwanese culture. In the regulations on street-food vendors, it is clearly established that street vendors shall maintain the cleanliness of their own stalls and must ensure that their food meets the officially established hygienic standards. Many other articles in the regulations have helped street vending to become more accepted by the general public as well as the shop owners that are their competition.[10]

According to Tourism Bureau of Taiwan, night markets have become the most popular tourist attraction in Taipei, even

---

10. "Regulations Governing Street Vendors of Taiwan Province," Laws & Regulations Database, The Republic of China, June 30, 1999, http://law.moj.gov.tw/Eng/LawClass/LawContent.aspx?pcODE=J0080027.

more attractive than the famous Taipei 101 Building and National Palace Museum, probably because of the delicious character.[11] This is just a further example of the connection between street food and the tourism industry of Taiwan.

Beef noodle soup, like many other Taiwanese street foods, has survived pretty well over the decades under the tolerance, protection and even promotion of Taiwanese government. Now it is definitely justified to call beef noodle soup "the National Noodle of Taiwan."

Conclusion

To those who do not know about the historical background of Chinese immigrants in Taiwan, Sichuan-flavored beef noodle soup can be easily misunderstood as a street food from Sichuan of Mainland China. It is indeed made in Taiwan, 100 percent authentic, by nostalgic Sichuan immigrants. Its success and general popularity in Taipei results also from the change of eating habits among Taiwanese, who used to see beef eating as taboo or luxury. With the efforts of the Taiwanese government to control the market price of food items, beef noodle soup can be sold at a cheap price and ordinary Taiwanese people can afford it. If it were not for the tolerance and protection of the Taiwanese government, beef noodle soup might not have been popular as street food in Taipei and would have remained confined to the menus of proper restaurants. Nowadays, beef noodle soup has been so undoubtedly popular in Taiwan that Taipei even endeavors to be the capital of beef noodle soup in the world by organizing a beef noodle soup festival.

---

11. "Revenue of Tourism Exceeds 100 Trillion USD in the Year of 2012 (100 Year of ROC)," Tourism Bureau, Republic of China (Taiwan), August 16, 2012, http://admin.taiwan.net.tw/news/news_d.aspx?no=249&d=3730&tag=2.

Bibliography

"40 Years Non-stop Business of Taiwanese Beef Noodle Soup Plans Its Marketing in Mainland China." NET EASE. September 1, 2010. Accessed January 2, 2015. http://news.163.com/10/0901/09/6F-G42A50000146BD.html?f=jsearch.

Gao, Wenqi. "Nostalgia through a Bowl of Beef Noodle." *New Economy*, no.27 (2013).

Gu, Jiaming. "The Connection of Military Dependents' Village to Beef Noodle in Taiwan." *Literature Life*, no. 9 (2012).

He, Shan. "Taiwan Opens the Beef Import from Canada for the Negotiations of TPP." Hong Kong China News Agency. January 17, 2014. http://www.hkcna.hk/content/2014/0117/238417.shtml.

Han, Yan. "Punishment for Butcher for Killing a Bull That Begs for Life." Buddhist Network of Xingtai. November 11, 2014. http://www.xtfj.org/xuefu/fujiaogushi/20140911/20780.html.

Jiang, Xian. "Taipei Beef Noodle: My Curiosity, Your Nostalgia." *History Reference*, no.22 (2012). Accessed October 26, 2014. http://wap.139sz.cn/read/article.php?id=246456&all=1.

Li, Ang. "Niurou mian/nouilles Au Boeuf." Sens-Public. November 14, 2008. http://www.sens-public.org/IMG/pdf/SensPublic_Li-Ang_roman.pdf.

Liang, Liang. "Beef Noodle." *China Newsweek*, no.27 (2008).

Liao, Xinzhong. "The Unknown Story of Waishengren (immigrants from Mainland China) in Taiwan." August 9, 2014. http://www.21ccom.net/articles/tgjj/2014/0809/110782_2.html.

Lu, Yaodong. "Where Does Beef Noodle Come From?" Taipei Beef Noodle Festival. October 12, 2005. http://www.tbnf.com.tw/m_know.htm.

Mengyu, Yang. "A Message from Taiwan: 'King of Beef Noodle Soup' in Taipei." BBC Chinese News. November 29, 2006. Accessed January 1, 2015. http://news.bbc.co.uk/chinese/simp/hi/newsid_6120000/newsid_6120700/6120790.stm.

Qian, Qi. "Beef Noodle in Taiwan." *Cooking Knowledge*, no.10 (2012).

"Regulations Governing Street Vendors of Taiwan Province." Laws & Regulations Database and The Republic of China. June 30, 1988. http://law.moj.gov.tw/Eng/LawClass/LawAll.aspx?PCode =J0080027.

"Report on International Religious Freedom." U.S. Department of State. October 26, 2009, http://www.state.gov/documents/organi- zation/132869.pdf.

Shu, Guozhi. *About Eating in Poverty: Stories about Food over the Past Fifty Years in Taiwan*. Taipei: Unitas Publishing, 2008.

Shu, Guozhi. *Notes on Street Food in Taipei*. Taipei: Crown Culture Corporation, 2007.

Sun, Zhijian. "'Marginal Administration' of Municipal Government: A Comparative Study on Regulations of Street Vendors" *Journal of Public Administration* 5, no. 3 (2012): 30-58.

Xu, Jianfeng. "Analysis of Change in Industrial Structure of Taiwan." *Taiwan Studies* 3 (2001).

Zhang, Wenjing. "Chat About Taiwan: Refusal of Beef." Blog of Zhang Wenjing, May 16, 2007. http://blog.sina.com.cn/s/ blog_4b1c7f9d010009id.html.

Eating London's Street Food, 1603-1714: Eel Pie, Pease Pottage and the Restoration

Emily Arthy

The idea to connect the phenomenon of street food with the unsensational topic of street dining in Stuart England at first sight seems like a very obscure choice. In seventeenth century England there was no food-to-go as we regularly observe in our daily lives today. There were no restaurants or takeaways, a means by which to eat the food was also lacking, equally there was no concrete food standards to which vendors were obliged to adhere. The lack of clean drinking water meant that beer was the beverage of choice of this period, with claret being enjoyed at lunchtime by the wealthy.

Surely with poverty so rife it is logical to think that Londoners were limited in their daily diet? Yet, from the outset of studying this topic of street food in the English capital at the time of the reign of the Stuarts, 1603-1714, such stereotypes and misconceptions are challenged. This article shows that the daily diet for Londoners of this time was surprisingly varied, rich in both protein and vitamins. It also paints a picture of a poor lower class that refused to accept poor quality food. This is in contrast to an emerging upper class that were experiencing the delights of French dining trends, exotic ingredients from the empire and culinary advancements such as the French invention of the two-pronged fork. London of the seventeenth century was a city of two halves divided by wealth, which to some extent intermingled in their daily lives—that is to say, two halves that were not yet geographically pigeonholed into their respective areas of east and west London. From the outset, it is clear that the two research questions will encompass factors which go beyond the preparation, sale, and consumption of food on London's streets.

Structurally this article is divided into three parts. First, the reader will be introduced to the basic geography of the locations mentioned. Second, examples of the Stuarts' street food will be presented along with the shifts their culinary choices brought about. In the third section, the notion of historical eating events will be explored, and in the final section, a conclusion will directly address the two research questions. These will again be considered in light of evidence found in secondary sources. In addition to that, the wider topic of migration will be considered and a brief evaluation made of exactly how this article adds to the diversity of this street food edited volume.

A Geographical Presentation of Seventeenth Century London: Market Traditions, Emerging Boroughs

The following map of London (Figure 1), although from approximately 1300, shows the Smithfield and Billingsgate markets, the Tower of London, and the location of Moorfields Park which Samuel Pepys, the Member of Parliament, English Naval Administrator and diarist, records in his diary in 1666 as an open park space. If we consider the River Thames as the most important entity of the city, a bird's eye view of London can be described in the following way: to the west on the south bank of the Thames is Lambethmoor, which is an open green space, to the west of the north bank to a significant degree in land is Smithfield meat market, Billingsgate market is located, directly on the river, on the north bank to the east. Its proximity to the river makes it clear why it emerged as a fish market at the end of the 1500s.

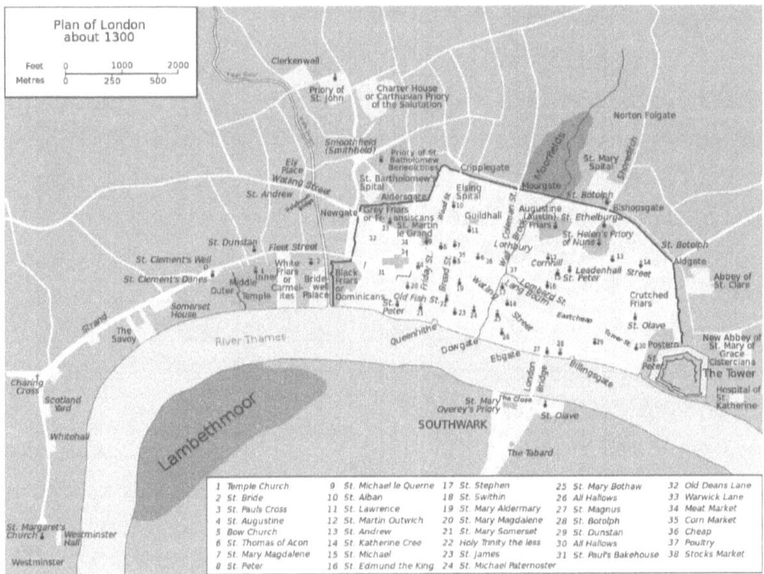

Figure 1. Map of London, 1300[1]

It is interesting to observe from this map and also from "A Country Man's Guide to the City," published 1653, that it is not easy to distinguish between areas of wealth and areas of poverty.[2] In seventeenth century London the way in which the rich lived in close proximity to the poor is a valid point to consider; however, there was a "gradual westward migration of the richer households."[3] This arguably marks the start of the East End—West End divide as we know it today. Christopher Hibbert continues to describe how today's affluent Westminster once included slums

<hr>

1. Grandiose, "Map of London, 1300," Licensed under CC BY-SA 3.0 via Wikimedia Commons, accessed January 15, 2015, http://commons.wikimedia.org/wiki/File:Map_of_London,_1300.svg#mediaviewer/File:Map_of_London,_1300.svg.
2. British Library Map of London, A Country Man's Guide to the City, 1653, accessed January 7, 2014, http://www.bl.uk/learning/images/changing/new/large5324.html.
3. Christopher Hibbert, *London: the Biography of a City* (London: Penguin Books, 1980), 55.

which were squalid and also typical of the city at this time.[4] Furthermore the names of streets such as 'Thieving Lane' indicate the crime which went hand in hand with poverty. However bad the situation was inside the walls of the city, outside, the activities of the highwaymen made the city seem relatively safe.

To the north of the city, open green spaces could be found only a stone's throw away from the chaos of Westminster—a balance which attracted the rich to build the best houses there.[5] London was also emerging at this time as a city which could easily be broken down into areas or boroughs of expertise. With the discipline of food history in mind, we can identify the poulterers of St George's, the millers of Stratford, and by the nineteenth century, a specialization of trade in the city which manifested itself in fine detail.[6]

London's Street Food 1603-1714, the State of the Urban Foodscape

Despite rife poverty, especially in the period prior to the Great Fire of the early 1660s, poor Londoners wanted to eat quality food. Even in Tudor England in 1562, the Venetian merchant, Alessandro Magno observed that "by then Londoners, even the poorer ones, had begun to shift their gastronomic focus from quantity to quality, leading the nation in the transition from brown bread to white and, in the following century, from pottage to pudding."[7]

The pie man became an institution in the history of London and its street food in Stuart times and provides further insight into the Stuarts' street food. Pies would be sold amid the general

---

4. Hibbert, *London: the Biography of a City*, 55.

5. Hibbert, *London: the Biography of a City*, 55.

6. Peter Ackroyd, *London: A Biography*, (London: Chatto & Windus, 2000), 126.

7. Richard Tames, *Feeding London: a Taste of History* (London: Historical Publications, 2003), 7.

hubbub of laborers, merchants, and gentry going about their daily business. Pies from the pie man would include proteins such as beef or mutton, fish including eels or fruit pies made from seasonal fruit.[8] The example of the pies available indicates that street food of this period offered a certain level of quality. The inclusion of a wider range of fruit, beyond the English apple, showed a departure from the Tudor suspicion towards fruit and vegetables.

On the topic of the provenance of London's street food, Carolyn Steele mentions the heritage of Norfolk turkeys being walked to the city annually since medieval times to meet the Christmas poultry demand.[9] Indeed Alessandro Magno poignantly commented back in 1562 that "it is almost impossible to believe that they could eat so much meat in one city alone."[10] Steele also identifies poultry which originated in Kent for sale at Borough market. Similarly, street hawkers offered London's poorest chicken and also rabbit meat to ensure their demand for meat was met.[11] With this point she also touches on the topic of migration; it was Irish game keepers who would bring their rabbits to sell in London in the autumn.

A further shift of this era was the emergence of a regionalization of English food specialties. An example if this are the Lilly white vinegar traders who were young men from the countryside, from the cider producing regions i.e. Somerset, who sold their vinegar on London's streets to prevent disease or for use in a culinary sauce.[12] In this period it seems that the countryman's affinity to his home county, typically in the English countryside, was never severed despite the establishment of his new urban life

8. Colin Spencer, *British Food: an Extraordinary Thousand Years of History* (New York: Columbia University Press, 2003), 263.

9. Carolyn Steele, *Hungry City: How Food Shapes our Lives* (London: Vintage Books, 2009), 119.

10. Tames, *Feeding London: a Taste of History*, 7.

11. Ackroyd, *London: a Biography*, 314.

12. Ackroyd, *London: a Biography*, 315.

in the English Capital. Those who moved to London to seek a better fortune may have lived in an urban setting, but still wanted to eat their country dishes.

In addition to that, traditional root vegetables, which were staples for countryside dwellers, remained staple foods for those who followed patterns of urban migration. Indeed, the popularity of country dining was very strong in England in general.[13] With regard to London's street food, it can also be viewed an extension of country eating, albeit against the backdrop of a chaotic urban space. The establishment of country gardening techniques within close proximity to the City is a strong legacy of the Stuart period and signified a level of self-sufficiency with regard to the mentioned root vegetables required for prominent street food dishes.[14] The topic of urban migration belongs to a wider topic of migration of this period which categorized by those 'English born' and 'non-English born' explains why with regard to food there was such a great demand for country dishes alongside a growing palette for more exotic ingredients.[15]

A recipe which reflects the English born elements of London society at this time is Pease pottage, a form of soup associated with the county of Sussex and the village after which it was named. It is a form of thick porridge consisting of peas, sugar, pepper, and occasionally mint. In the countryside, bacon was added to the mixture if it was available and the pease pudding was gently boiled in a pudding cloth, which was invented in the seventeenth century.[16] Pease pottage could be purchased in cook shops on the streets

---

13. Stephen Mennell, *All Manners of Food, Eating and Taste in England and France from the Middle Ages to the Present* (Oxford: Basil Blackwell, 1986), 130.
14. Tames, *Feeding London: a Taste of History*, 80.
15. Jacob Selwood, *Diversity and Difference in Early Modern London* (Farnham: Ashgate Publishing Limited, 2010), 122.
16. Alan Davidson, *The Oxford Companion to Food* (Oxford: Oxford Univ. Press 1999), 591.

of London. Those purchased at cook shops constituted a meal in and of themselves and were nutritionally balanced.[17]

The increasing demand for more exotic food commodities in the city of London can be attributed to the success of the British East India Company (EIC) and the influence of the non-English born. As Richard Tames, a lecturer and certified London Blue Badge tourist guide, writes: "The buoyant expansion of overseas trade with tropical countries enabled the affluent to buy such luxury ingredients as sugar, pepper, ginger or currants in larger quantities at lower prices."[18] In Stuart England, with regard to London's street food, this culinary expansion to exotic ingredients gradually manifested itself on the streets of the capital.

One example of this is sugar. Evidence of the growing demand for this exotic ingredient can be found in the English recipe for cake as was known in the medieval era compared to that of the seventeenth century. *The Oxford Companion to Food* pinpoints the 1660s as the decade where usage of sugar instead of honey became a common ingredient in cake recipes. [19] This was due to sugar's falling price, a circumstance which stemmed directly from the successful exploitation of slave labor in the Caribbean and increasing quantities on the British mainland. The first attempt to grow a pineapple on English shores in 1661 also signified the influence exotic food had on the palette of seventeenth century Londoners.[20] Finally the eventual adding of curry spices to the East End dish "jellied eels" is an indication of culinary influences specifically from India which would only be formally penned in a recipe by Hannah Glasse in her cookbook one century later.[21]

---

17. Spencer, *British Food*, 149.
18. Tames, *Feeding London: a Taste of History*, 17.
19. Davidson, *The Oxford Companion to Food*, 123.
20. Davidson, *The Oxford Companion to Food*, 609.
21. Davidson, *The Oxford Companion to Food*, 236.

Eating History: the Connection between Turbulent Events and the Consumption of Street Food

The English Civil War, 1642–51, brought about a circumstance which would cause fear in any monarchical nation: an internal rebellion against the crown. This event was so dividing, so engulfing, and so deeply felt at all levels of English life that it is no surprise to discover that London's street food of the mid-seventeenth century takes on a rather Puritan twist. Of course, not everyone appreciated the influence Puritanism had on food and so hidden recipe books including foods which were prohibited or deemed immoral had a high value.[22] With Oliver Cromwell at the helm of the English Commonwealth strict rules had to be adhered to. Feast days were turned into fast days, the consumption of alcohol was restricted, and in 1644 parliament even passed a bill effectively banning Christmas—or more specifically the consumption of mince pies and plum puddings, a ruling which technically still stands today.[23]

With the memory of modest eating as a very recent event, the Restoration to the English throne in 1660 of Charles II signified a revival in the grandeur of English cookery, as seen in the royal courts of Charles I before the Civil War. Charles II spent the duration of the English Commonwealth in exile in France and so French influences can strongly be identified in Restoration cooking and of course in London street food. The notion of London's poor also wanting to take part in the culinary trends set by the upper class demonstrates another manner in which they refused to regress back to the diet of a peasant. The example of the pie shows how both the poor and rich could share in versions of the same dish. In the BBC documentary *The Supersizers go Restoration*, the

---

22. Spencer, *British Food*, 137.
23. Ian Crofton, *A Curious History of Food and Drink* (London: Querus, 2013), 109.

pie was prominent in upper class dining and in street food consumption alike. The upper classes would be entertained with the theatre of a grand pie with a rich plethora of meats while back on the street it was a good way to preserve meat over multiple days.[24] It would not be until the mid-nineteenth century that the role of the pie seller would all be but become extinct due to the success of the pie shops.[25] The pie seller on the streets of London was the cornerstone of seventeenth century city life.

By 1665, the year in which the final episode of the bubonic plague broke out, London was a city of clearly defined contrasts of "hunger and prodigality, filth and luxury, a boudoir next to a dung hill."[26] The poor fared particularly badly in this year. With regard to food there were such ideas on the streets of London that certain foods could prevent one from the unavoidable death the bubonic plague would bring. Ian Crofton writes in his book *A Curious History of Food and Drink* that Londoners were convinced that onions somehow prevented the spread of the plague because according to their observation onion sellers never suffered from the deadly disease.[27] It would be a logical conclusion therefore to assume that onion sales on the streets of London flourished in a time largely of decline. The onion gives just one example of the connection of prevailing events in the city of London and food history and also reflects the still strong medieval influence of food as medicine—another reason to explain why a livelihood could be made from the sale of individual food commodities on the streets of seventeenth century London.

---

24. British Broadcasting Corporation, "The Supersizers go Restoration," BBC Documentary, originally broadcast in 2008, YouTube video series, compiled by "Johanna Z," April 21, 2014, www.youtube.com/watch?v=TCfx-98Ei5lM&list=PLXeZYHWmm_iCNLKjsSrk0VVdQLI8WaHxa.

25. Spencer, *British Food*, 263.

26. James Leasor, *The Plague and the Fire* (London: James Leasor Ltd, 2011), 4.

27. Crofton, *A Curious History of Food and Drink*, 118.

In September 1666, the Great Fire of London broke out. The starting point of the fire was indeed in a place where street food was produced, a bakery. It was Thomas Farriner's bakery in Pudding Lane where the flames first ignited. Anecdotal evidence suggests the name of this street was due to the cattle market there and meat puddings sold. Pudding Lane was also surrounded by warehouses which contained highly flammable goods such as timber, rope and oil.[28] Of the fire Samuel Pepys recounts in his diary how he initially went to the Tower of London in order to gain information on the mysterious blaze. He makes reference to a Fish Street in close proximity to Pudding Lane, a further example of how connected to food the city of London is.

With regard to street food, we can pick up his diary again in the aftermath of the fire. On the 8th September, 1666, just three days after the Great Fire was extinguished Samuel Pepys indicates that London's street food was emerging from the ashes: "I bought two eeles upon the Thames, cost me six shillings."[29] Pepys indicates suspicion of arson committed by foreign revolutionaries as a common fear among Londoners. He continues to express his concern for the safety of his Parmesan cheese and claret in light of the fire coming in very close proximity of his house. In this way he reflects his upper class social heritage and indicates that he had access to food stuffs that were not readily available on the street. For the working class and poor the fire had a direct effect on their

28. Museum of London, "London's Burning: the Great Fire of London 1666," exhibition archive online, 2005, accessed November 29, 2014, http://archive.museumoflondon.org.uk/MuseumOfLondon/Templates/microsites/generic/HomePage_alt.aspx?NRMODE=Published&NRNODEGUID={43DE1A8E-319E-426E-AF0F-A85F08A16029}&NRORIGINALURL=percent2FLondons-Burningpercent2F&NRCACHEHINT=NoModifyGuest.

29. Samuel Pepys, 1893, *Diary of Samuel Pepys*, Project Gutenberg online, last updated October 2012, http://www.gutenberg.org/files/4200/4200-h/4200-h.htm.

street food. Pepys describes how the price of bread, among those thousands displaced after the fire who sought shelter in Moorfields Park, doubled.[30] It would be a valid conclusion to assume this was the case as well with pies, soups, and puddings.

Summary

The first reflective point to make in this brief study on street food of Stuart London is the fact that it was so intertwined into daily urban life that it was not viewed or categorized as a separate entity. As we today would tend to use the facilities of our private kitchens to feed ourselves, the Stuarts sought the nearest pie sellers, meat, fish hawkers, or warm puddings of the cook shops to satisfy their hunger. The fact that this activity took place on the street is not considered unusual in the literature. Samuel Pepys' diary is a particularly useful primary source because it gives an insight into both the dining habits of the poor man or woman on London's streets and beyond into the private dining rooms of the growing upper class. Pepys witnessed the selling of eels on the banks of the Thames as well as enjoying the more exotic food this transitionary era in English eating fashioned. A most fitting example is how he mentions indulging in chocolate at breakfast time instead of ale. [31]

The River Thames can be viewed as a critical entity in the process of culinary change taking place in England at this time. Similarly, the strong theme of migration from the countryside to London established country eating habits as the norm for poorer classes. Slowly, more exotic foods appeared alongside or were added to what had been typically country recipes and foods. The concept of the specialization of regional foods in England was also increasingly evident on the streets of London. London became a

---

30. Pepys, 1893, *Diary of Samuel Pepys.*
31. Spencer, *British Food,* 153.

microcosm for the diverse way in which many of England's counties were specializing in regional foods.

A further poignant point of conclusion relates to the lower classes of London society: they were not willing to submit to a diet of bread and beer alone, despite lacking the wealth to own a private kitchen. It is fascinating how the lower echelons of society wanted to follow the eating trends of Restoration England, for example, and normalized the consumption of certain meats, white bread and pies. This is surprising when one considers food prices, which in general were climbing over the course of the seventeenth century.

At the other end of the hierarchy, the culinary influences of the upper classes should not be ignored. After the Restoration this focused on elaborate French cuisine with theatre served with each meal and to some extent can be interpreted as a strong affirmation of the reinstatement of the English monarchy. The trends, which the upper classes set for more exotic ingredients such as sugar, affected foodstuffs not exclusively consumed by those of noble backgrounds. Therefore it was in following such food trends set by the upper classes that the lower classes' eating habits also changed. The influence of the East India Company officials' taste for the Indian curry in the seventeenth century saw the opening of the first Indian restaurant in London in the following century. The poorer classes also showed their taste for curry with small amounts of spice being added to dishes familiar to them such as jellied eels.

Conclusion

In directly addressing the first research question the following conclusions can be made. The Stuart influence on London's street food was unique in the way it firmly installed country food habits as the basis for street food in the English capital. The country food influence expanded to not only include ingredients which in the Tudor period had been viewed with suspicion but also to include ingredients which were of global provenance. The daily interaction of the upper and lower classes in London's streets during this period, as Pepys' diary verifies, enables the Stuart period to maybe be viewed as the last time period in which the eating habits of the upper class could directly influence the lower class to such an extent. Victorian London would witness the firm establishment of the poorer East End and richer West End.

From a brief investigation into the notion of eating historical events, the following conclusions can be made. Firstly, the connection between the Puritan politics of Cromwell's Protectorate and the general consensus of dissatisfaction with his prohibitions concerning food is very evident in the literature. To establish connections between less food-orientated topics such as the Great Fire of London, apart from the fact that it started in a bakery, the task is more demanding. From the use of Pepys' diary, however, the connection between the fire and London's street food is made more concrete. Similarly the effects of the bubonic plague on London's street food scene can be observed in the demand for certain medicinal foods. Further study could investigate London's street food post 1666 with a view to establish to what extent the reforms brought about after the fire did to improve hygiene standards.

Finally, with regard to the topic of migration, which arguably binds this whole topic together, if the finer details of migration to London during the approximate hundred year period were to be further examined, there is strong evidence to denote that the street food history of more specific minority groups could in turn be told. This could be a history of Jewish street food in the East End, the influence on the city's street food of the establishment of China town or indeed the influence of Indian eating trends brought back by the East India Company.

Bibliography

British Broadcasting Corporation. "The Supersizers go Restoration" BBC Documentary, originally broadcast in 2008. YouTube video series, compiled by "Johanna Z." April 21, 2014. www.youtube.com/watch?v=TCfx98Ei5lM&list=PLXeZYHWmm_iCNLKjsS-rk0VVdQLI8WaHxa.

Ackroyd, Peter. *London: A biography*. London: Chatto & Windus, 2000.

———. *The Great Fire of London*. London: Penguin Books, 1993.

Crofton, Ian. *A Curious History of Food and Drink*. London: Querus, 2013.

Davidson, Alan. *The Oxford Companion to Food*. Oxford: Oxford Univ. Press 1999.

Hibbert, Christopher. *London: the Biography of a City*. London: Penguin Books, 1980.

Leasor, James. *The Plague and the Fire*. London: James Leasor Ltd, 2011.

Mennell, Stephen. *All Manners of Food: Eating and Taste in England and France from the Middle Ages to the Present*. Illinois: Univ. Illinois Press, 1996.

Museum of London. "London's Burning: the Great Fire of London 1666." exhibition archive online. 2005. accessed November 29, 2014. http://archive.museumoflondon.org.uk/MuseumOfLondon/Templates/microsites/generic/HomePage_alt.aspx?NRMODE=Published&NRNODEGUID={43DE1A8E-319E-426E-AF0F-A85F-08A16029}&NRORIGINALURL=percent2FLondons-Burningpercent2F&NRCACHEHINT=NoModifyGuest.

Pepys, Samuel. 1893. *The Diary of Samuel Pepys*, Project Gutenberg online. Last updated October 2012. http://www.gutenberg.org/cache/epub/3331/pg3331.html.

Porter, Roy. *London: A Social History*, London: Hamilton, 1994.

Selwood, Jacob. *Diversity and Difference in Early Modern London*. Farnham: Ashgate Publishing Limited, 2010.

Spencer, Colin. *British Food: an Extraordinary Thousand Years of History*.

New York: Columbia University Press, 2003.

Steele, Carolyn. *Hungry City: How Food shapes our Lives*. London: Vintage Books, 2009.

Tames, Richard. *Feeding London: a Taste of History*. London: Historical Publications, 2003.

Index

A

Anderson, Benedict, 99

Appadurai, Arjun, 25, 74, 75, 94; hybridization, 13, 14, 25, 91, 94, 104

Arabia, 29–34

Ashkenazi, 62

Austria, 14, 48, 91–104, 107–117, 119; GastarbeiterInnen demographics, 97; immigrant stereotypes, 102; immigrants in mass media, 109, 114; immigration from Turkey, 97; immigration from Yugoslavia, 108; integration of migrants, 98, 101; post-war, 91–99, 101-102

B

Baja, 79, 81

Baklava, 66

Balkan, 107, 109, 111–112, 114–117, 119; Balkan-Grill, 109, 111–118; Balkanism, 114; Bohemia, 112; Croatia, 112; food tastes, 117; in European discourse, 114; Serbia, 112; Slovenia, 113

Bautista, Oscar, 86

beans, 81

beef, 81, 108, 152, 163–173

beef noodle soup, 163–173

Bell, Glen, 75

Bhimji, Fazila, 82

Bion, Wilfred Ruprecht, 64

Bourdieu, Pierre, 64

bread, 80, 95, 99, 152, 137, 148, 152, 180; druze pita, 66; simit, 32

Buddhism: eating habits, *See* Taiwan: attitude toward beef

bureaucracy, 82; challenges, 108

burrito, 73, 79, 81, 82

C

California, 67, 74, 78–82
Cal-Mex, 77, 78, 80
canned beef, 166, 167
chalupa, 73
cheese, 81, 95, 151
chicken, 81, 85, 138, 151, 152, 181
chili, 75, 77, 81, 166, 167
Choi, Roy, 85
cod, 48
corn, 48, 73, 138; Cuitlacoche (corn smut), 21
couscous, 55, 66
culinary tourism: in recipe books, 74
cultural invasion, *See* United States: Americanization
Currywurst, 38

E

eating habits, 15, 17, 18, 51, 54, 55, 57, 63, 84, 88, 115, 118, 145, 147, 148, 158, 163, 168, 170, 173, 187–189; adaptation, 74, 78, 91; as opposed to eating preferences, 57; as symbol of socioeconomic status, 172; dissemination within society, 104; introduction of new cuisines, 86; logistic influences, 81; national, 51, 54; religious proscription, 63; take-away food, 152; urbanization, 132
egg, 81
elote, 73
empalme, 73
enchilada, 80, 82
ethnic food, 36, 37, 51–57, 66, 74, 77, 87; consumers, 53, 54, 56, 57, 77

F

Falafel, 66, 67–69, 101,
fast food, 39, 75, 81, 82, 84, 85, 87, 101

food safety: consumers, 137

food truck, 83, 86, 138, 79, 145, 146, 153–157

foreigner, 40, 48, 50, 97, 98

FremdarbeiterInnen, *See* GastarbeiterInnen

Freud, Sigmund, 49, 61, 62, 65; fetish, 61–65, 69

fusion, 86

G

GastarbeiterInnen, 97, 104; conflict with other immigrant groups, 98; cultural segregation, 104; from Turkey, 97, 99, 109; from Yugoslavia, 97, 107–110; immigrant demographics, 160; legal restrictions, 110; polemic use, 111; policy history, 104; political correctness, 58; program history, 110; program structure, 110; racism, 108; street markets, 99

Gecekondu, *See* Istanbul: informal housing

global studies, 17; global history, 17, 18

globalization, 20

gordita, 73

guacamole, 81

guest workers, *See* GastarbeiterInnen

Gvion, Liora, 67

H

Habsburg Empire, 91, 96, 108, 112, 113

Haredim, 63

hot dog, 33, 37–39; origin in the U.S., 37

hummus, 13, 61–63, 65, 67–70

Hungary, 60

I

ice cream, 66

identity: as fetish, 61; culinary, 69, 80, 108, 131; differentiation, 84; ethnic marker, 47–50, 58, 59; ethno-narcissism, 49, 50, 64; homogeneity, 52; hybridization, 91; large group, 49, 50; narcissism, 49; nationalism, 49, 81;

othering, 104; political construction, 112; preserved in food, 119; secularism, 30; social legitimacy, 66; symbols in media, 63
Imagined Communities, 99
Islam, 103
Israel, 61–70; zionism, 32, 33
Istanbul, 125–140; chain migration, 130, 133, 139; economic development, 83; foreign direct investment, 127; iconic dishes, 70; informal housing, 132, 133; population of, 126; street food culture, 127; vendor registration, 128

J

Jewish, 62, 63, 66, 67, 69, 70, 189,

K

Kebab, 14, 27, 37, 77, 91, 92, 94, 99, 100–104

L

Latinos, 85
lettuce, 81
London, 135, 177–189; urban planning, 139
Los Angeles, 73–88, 139, 154; First Street Mercado, 77

M

Marx, Karl, 65
Mauss, Marcel, 18, 44
Mexican American, 73–78, 80–82, 84, 87, 88
Mexico, 77, 80, 81, 83, 84, 86, 152,
migration: cultural invasion, 40; unemployment, 171
military provision, 33

N

nationalism, 37, 49, 81, 134, 137

native, 40, 53–58, 80, 98, 104, 163, 164, 168, 170

neo-nomadism, 9

New York City, 18

Norway, 138, 145–160; cuisine, 158; Oslo, 151–159; Swedish migration to, 159; traditional dishes, 148

nuts, 66

O

onion, 81, 185

orange, 48

orange juice, 138

Ottoman Empire, 91, 94, 114, 126, 128

P

Palestine, 66, 67

Pilcher, Jeffrey M., 74, 79

pizza, 39, 40, 66, 101, 102, 147, 151, 158

pork, 81, 85, 108, 152, 171

potato, 48, 148

R

recipe, 28, 39, 48, 77, 80, 86, 148, 182–184, 187

refugees, 135

restaurant: diversity, 136; ethnic, 52; financial investment, 126; gendered space, 33; growth of consumer culture, 86; market growth, 126; online food vending, 131; pricing, 155; pricing trends, 157; traditional, 53

Robertson, Roland: glocalization, 25

S

Said, Edward, 93; Orientalism, 93, 114

sambusak, 66

San Diego, 78

San Francisco, 78, 80

sandwich, 73, 80

sausage, 85, 95

Smith, Andrew, 74, 81

soup, 73, 163

Spain, 47–59, 80, 109

spatialization, 25

spinach, 48

Spinoza, Baruch, 61

street food: as opposed to restaurants, 73, 75, 77, 78, 83, 91–95, 99, 100; commercialization, 85; conservative opinion, 26; consumer choice, 170; consumers, 118; definition, 19; etiquette, 27; fusion, 77; globalization, 126; government promotion, 149; health hazard, 70; hygiene, 28; in post-war society, 119; legality, 70; military provision, 33; names, *See* Appadurai, Arun: hybridization; public image, 25; regulation, 18, 22, 28, 35, 36, 47, 51, 128, 131, 149, 156, 163, 164, 171, 172; served in restaurants, 107; social class, 24; social space, 13; sold in restaurants, 128; supply chain, 21; symbol of home, 119; vendor, 23, 65, 66, 68, 76–78, 81–85, 108, 116, 118, 119, 127–131, 135, 138, 164, 171, 172; vendor background, 20, 130

sunflower seeds, 66

sushi, 85

<h1 style="text-align:center">T</h1>

taco, 14, 73–88, 151, 156

Tahini, 67

Taipei, 139, 145, 163–173; night market, 172

Taiwan, 163–173; agriculture, mechanization, 170; attitude toward beef, 169, 170; dining habits, 187; food market controls, 160; XE, 90, 91, 93, 95, 96

tamale, 21, 73, 80

Tarlabaşı, 127, 130, 134

Texas, 80

Tex-Mex, 77, 78, 80

tlayuda, 73

tomato, 48, 81

torta, 73

tortilla, 73, 75, 79–82, 85

tostada, 73

tourism: and urban planning, 139; as motivation for policy, 149; culinary, 73, 74, 76–80; street food, 131

Turkey, 93, 97, 99, 109, 125–127, 132, 134, 136, 137, 150; (PKK) Kurdistan Workers' Party, 127; Ankara, 128, 129; economy, 126; internal migration, 126; Kurdish migration, 127; policy of assimilation, 134; Tarlabaşı, 135

U

United Nations, 19

United States, 74, 81; Americanization, 40, 74; domestic tourism, 43; ethnic food in, 74, 77; guest workers, 107

urbanization, 132, 134

V

Vienna: Turkish Immigrants, 92

Volkan, Vamık D., 64

W

wheat, 79, 81

Würstelstand, 91–104, 108, 109, 119

X

xenophobia, 18, 26

Y

Yugoslavia, 97, 107–119; Socialist Federal Republic of, 109

www.ingramcontent.com/pod-product-compliance
Lightning Source LLC
Chambersburg PA
CBHW031108250726
48655CB00004B/1624